D0887844

A CHARMED *Rock 'N' Roll* LIFE

ROBIN LE MESURIER

WITH ANDY MERRIMAN

The Book Guild Ltd

First published in Great Britain in 2017 by
The Book Guild Ltd
9 Priory Business Park
Wistow Road, Kibworth
Leicestershire, LE8 0RX
Freephone: 0800 999 2982
www.bookguild.co.uk
Email: info@bookguild.co.uk
Twitter: @bookguild

Cover photographs © Stéphane de Bourgies

Typeset in Sabon MT

Printed and bound in Great Britain by CPI Group (UK) Ltd, Croydon, CR0 4YY

ISBN 978 1910878 866

British Library Cataloguing in Publication Data.
A catalogue record for this book is available from the British Library.

MIX
Paper from
responsible sources
FSC® C013604

I've been thinking and procrastinating about writing this book for some time, but got nudged so many times from friends and family that I'd thought I would finally put my fingers to a keyboard and try and recall what I could. So I hope, dear readers, that you can follow and understand my ramblings and enjoy them as much as I enjoyed remembering them and putting them to paper.

This book is dedicated to my wife Jules Le Mesurier, my wicked stepmother Joan Le Mesurier, my parents, my brother Jake Le Mesurier, and everyone who has been a part of my most interesting life. Thank you all.

CONTENTS

A Knight of the Realm and yours truly (PENNY LANCASTER)

FOREWORD

I have to put it very frankly to you my friends, I find Robin Le Mesurier a complete and utter bore. I have had better conversations with a dining table. Also, my friends, he can't play guitar for sausage and was always late for concerts, turning up drunk and out of tune.

If you believe that then you'll believe I am still 26.

During my expansive and illustrious career I have had many wonderful and creative guitarists in my band, but Robin was always just a cut above, a beautiful soulful lead, driving rhythms like a locomotive. And an unforgettable stage presence.

Over the years I have had some wonderful musicians and bands but it is simply not enough to be a fine musician. I always wanted mates, someone I could sit at the bar with, someone I could fall down with, even someone I could confide in. Robin has all of these qualities and more as a fully paid up member of the 'Sex Police' (please refer to my book *Rod the Autobiography* on sale near you), in charge and responsible for the organisation of all sorts of shenanigans and tomfoolery.

Robin like myself was born to be 'a Rocker', I mean just look at the two of us. Can you imagine either of us working in Sainsburys? Not that there's anything wrong with working in Sainsburys, of course. We were, I suppose, cast by the good Lord.

Robin and I are still very good mates and we see each other on a regular basis and I sincerely hope our friendship survives after his read of this backward, I mean foreword...

SIR ROD STEWART CBE

PREFACE

Earl's Court, London 1965. A twelve-year-old boy is in the kitchen of his family home in Eardley Crescent. The house is, as usual, full of visitors and friends – and he'd been woken in the small hours by Peter Sellers and Spike Milligan jamming. It was the sort of thing that happened quite regularly in his house, which was often full of actors, musicians and entertainers. He loves the lively, bohemian and warm atmosphere in which the house basks. The boy cranes his neck out of the window to see hordes of people making their way to the Exhibition Centre and concert hall. He dreams of playing there one day.

June 1983. Nearly twenty years later, and the same boy is grown up and thrilled. The boy, well it's me… that much, I suppose, is obvious… and I am now a member of the Rod Stewart band. I'm backstage at Earl's Court, not having changed yet, just visiting with friends and chatting with Dad and Jake. It's quite a sprawling area covered in Astro Turf, a bar, of course, and much food. There are a number of dressing rooms plus a warm-up room for the band to go through a couple of raucous songs to get in the mood. I change into my stage clothes – an electric blue suit and sneakers.

Elton John told me I looked 'just fantastic darling', which was comforting.

We climb the steps to the stage and assume the usual positions, myself stage right as usual, behind a red velvet curtain, emblazoned with the capitals 'RS' in huge gold lettering. We can't see the audience but can hear their 'buzz'. They are clearly eager and expectant, whistling and shouting for the show to start. I'm very excited, but not nervous. We launch into the intro to 'Tonight I'm Yours', and the curtain immediately splits from the middle, opening wide to reveal a stark white design with Rod centre stage and the band already rocking. We play twenty songs to a vociferous and appreciative audience for over two hours and end the gig with 'Sailing' before two encores. We leave the stage with the crowd still screaming for more.

That night was really special for me. My brother Jake was there as was my proud dad and lots of friends in the audience including Elton, Jeff Beck, and many others. My mum had died nearly three years previously, but I felt her presence. Yes, she wouldn't have missed this for the world. My dream had come true.

1

NATIONAL TREASURES

In the early morning hours of Sunday 22nd March 1953, after nine months of solitary confinement (with no time off for good behaviour), my mother released me to the care of The Princess Beatrice Hospital on the corner of Old Brompton Road and Warwick Road in Earl's Court, London – about five hundred yards from where I grew up and lived for twenty-seven years or so.

It's a miracle I actually made it at all. While pregnant, my mum, actress Hattie Jacques, was appearing in the BBC radio comedy *Educating Archie* and was also directing and appearing in a Players' Theatre revue in London, *The Bells of St Martins*. In one sketch, she had to slide energetically down a table, ending up doing 'the splits'. After each performance – especially towards the end of the run – the cast, aware of her pregnant state, looked on nervously, checking that she was in the pink. Fortunately for me, if not the cast, the show closed earlier than expected, which was something of a relief to my dad, who, despite his laid back nature, was becoming increasingly nervous about Mum's exertions. Hattie and my dad, John Le Mesurier, also an actor, were apparently pretty relaxed about my impending arrival and would take day trips in their Morris Minor and enjoy outings to the theatre and cinema right up until her hospitalisation.

Although this was during the era when fathers were first encouraged to attend the birth of their offspring, my father was noticeably absent at the labour ward, which was probably a relief to Mum and the nursing staff. In fact he spent the evening of 22nd March 1953 knocking back the booze in the company of actor Denis Shaw who, according to Dad, 'reserved his most memorable performances for the saloon bar'.

Someone from the hospital rang the next morning to let Dad know that I had been born. He dropped in to greet me and described his reaction to me as being 'enchanted'. I can just imagine him offering a casual 'jolly well done' to my pale and exhausted mother before going off to celebrate.

Apart from my own birth, which didn't create much of a splash, 1953 was quite eventful. It was the year of the Coronation of Queen Elizabeth II, Edmund Hillary and Sherpa Tenzing were the first people to reach the summit of Mount Everest and Ian Fleming published his first James Bond novel, *Casino Royale*. My timing was also impeccable in that the rationing of sweets had ended the month before my birth. Frankie Laine, Perry Como and Guy Mitchell dominated the pop charts and classic movies, such as *Roman Holiday, From Here to Eternity* and *Shane* were released.

My first home was the family house at 67 Eardley Crescent, a four storey whitewashed Victorian house, owned by my maternal grandmother, Mary Jacques and described by my dad as 'a comfortable, if rambling, pile with more stairs than were strictly necessary'. A walled back garden led straight on to the rear of Earl's Court Exhibition Centre, which some of the rooms also overlooked and the house was situated just on the bend of the street, consequently making all the rooms in the house slightly skewiff.

To my dismay the iconic building is to be replaced by a residential and retail site and demolition has already started. I have such fond memories of the hall from an early age. There was an act playing there at one point – I can't remember who it was, but Mum noticed how many people were queuing down our street in awful weather and she decided to make tea for as many of them as possible. I helped her and I will never forget the look of astonishment of the punters receiving hot tea from Hattie Jacques. But, that was her. She was all heart. An amazing woman.

But I'm getting ahead of myself. Let me introduce some of my family members... Hattie originally hailed from Sandgate – she was either a woman of Kent or a Kentish woman – I've never quite known the difference. In fact, Hattie wasn't even known as 'Hattie' at this early stage in her life. She was given the endearing and lasting nickname twenty years later so on the 18th February 1922 in Folkestone, the birth was registered in her real name of Josephine Edwina Jaques and she was known to family and close friends as 'Jo'. (The 'c' was added later as a nod in the direction of the more fashionable French derivation.)

Hattie's mother, Mary, had met my grandfather, the rather grandly named Robin Rochester Jaques while he was in the services and she was a nurse. Mary's own father was Joseph Edwin Thorn, who owned a jeweller's shop and pawnbrokers. His wife, Adelaide, Hattie's grandmother, was the daughter of William Brown, a deceased East End cheesemonger, and his widow, Hannah, was thought to be of Jewish descent.

On her father's side, Hattie's grandfather, Joseph Rochester Jaques, a billiard room manager, was born in Northumberland and his wife, Hattie's other grandmother Flora, was born in Dartmouth, Devon, the daughter of a Newton Abbot bookseller.

My paternal grandfather Robin Jaques had previously served in the army before enlisting in the Royal Air Force. He was an extremely dashing and excellent athlete, who had hopes of becoming a professional footballer, representing both the army and the Royal Air Force at the highest levels. Originally living in Kent, the family, which now included Hattie and her elder brother, also named Robin, were uprooted to RAF Spittlegate in Lincolnshire. Flying Officer Jaques joined 100 Squadron and soon embarked on flying lessons in an Avro 504, which had been used in the early stages of the First World War for light bombing and reconnaissance missions.

Unfortunately the move to Lincolnshire proved to have tragic consequences. In August 1923, less than two months after he had moved to Spittlegate and the family had settled in the nearby town of Newton, my grandfather took a solo flight in his Avro, but lost control while attempting some aerial gymnastics. The plane crashed to the ground. A local newspaper described the scene: 'Flight Lieutenant Jaques lay dead just clear of the machine, his skull being smashed and neck broken and other injuries. He must have struck the ground with tremendous force. Death was instantaneous.' (In August 2015 a service of dedication took place in Grantham cemetery and a headstone erected on Grandad's previously unmarked grave. A fly-past by a solitary Spitfire in his honour commemorated his death a year later).

3

My dashing grandfather, Robin Rochester Jaques (JOHN PAUL JACQUES)

The impact on the family, which then consisted of Hattie aged eighteen months and her brother Robin, aged three, was dreadful and prompted a move to London. The Jaques' were fatherless, almost destitute, and faced a very bleak future. Mary left Lincolnshire almost immediately and moved in with her parents, Joseph and Adelaide Thorn, who occupied a flat above their shop in King's Road, Chelsea.

Thankfully this move to London proved lifesaving. Not only did the prosperous Joseph and Adelaide provide financial security, but more telling, the sanctuary of an extremely happy home life. The children were raised in what Hattie later described as 'a fairytale existence' and the shop at night as 'an Aladdin's cave… the illuminated windows glittering with colourful gems and silver and gold bracelets'. It was here that Hattie gained her first experiences of live theatre as Mary, who had actually trodden the boards herself, took her daughter to a plethora of West End shows.

In later years my brother and I were always really, really close to Mary, which was in stark contrast to our relationship with Dad's parents. There was surprisingly little contact between us and our paternal grandparents in Bury St Edmunds' – in fact we had very little to do with them. They were almost strangers and my brother and I hardly ever saw them. They seemed very far removed. In fact my dad's dad seemed even more reclusive than my dad! He was very difficult to get to open up, at least as far as my brother and I were concerned. I always found my grandfather rather severe. He wouldn't brook any nonsense, let's put it that way.

Dad had always said that he had never got to know his own father very well. He was a lawyer, who wanted to become a Conservative politician and was out most evenings at meetings and party events. He was much closer to his mother, Amy, who I remember as being very warm, loving and comforting. Dad had been sent to boarding school at the age of nine, which, in later life, he described as 'somewhat surprising' – both of them being 'sensitive people'. He went initially to Grenham House in Kent and then to Sherborne school in Dorset. He hated both institutions, disliking the snobbishness, narrowness of thinking and bullying. He resented Sherborne for 'its closed mind, its collective capacity for rejecting anything that did not conform to the image of manhood as portrayed in the ripping yarns of a scouting manual'. He admitted he was something of a loner at school, which may explain some of his diffident behaviour which has also affected me. At least I think it has…

Like Mum, Dad had already developed an interest in the theatre and as a child he had also been taken regularly to West End shows. His father wanted him to follow in his footsteps in the legal profession, but that didn't really interest Dad and, in his mid 20's, he decided to become an actor, adopting his mother's maiden name of Le Mesurier.

Mum's first professional engagement as a singer and comedienne was in 1944 at The Players' Theatre in London – the venue which was to play a huge part in her professional and personal life. The Players' productions were famed for music hall turns in Victorian style and right from her debut, Hattie established a reputation as being the Players' most popular entertainer. In the summer of 1947, Dad was introduced to the Players' by an actor friend. He loved the unique atmosphere of the theatre and in his autobiography, *A Jobbing Actor*, wrote, 'One of the leading lights was a remarkable girl called Hattie Jacques. She was bright and witty and vivacious and an entertainer to her fingertips… on that first evening I was quickly caught up with Hattie's ebullient good humour and sense of anarchic fun'.

Dad returned a few times and after one show, asked Hattie for a drink. Within a few days, Hattie introduced Dad to Bruce Copp, one of Mum's closest friends, telling him, 'I've met this man who's rather special'. He, in turn, found her irresistible, which was flattering to Mum, who had always been self conscious of her shape. He described her in admiring terms, 'Hattie made a virtue of size. She wore long, billowy dresses, often very revealing. It was as if knowing she was bound to be noticed, she wanted to make a real job of it. It was characteristic of her that on visits to Covent Garden, she outmatched the sartorial splendour of the wealthier clientele by enveloping herself in a black, swirling highwayman's cloak borrowed from the Players' wardrobe'.

Dad was separated from but actually still married to his actress wife, June Melville, who was very beautiful, cultured, elegant and engaging – at least until about the fourth cocktail when, according to Bruce Copp, she became 'less articulate, her make-up smudged, her elegant hat slipped to a jaunty angle and her mink stole slipped off her shoulders'.

Although Dad maintained a bachelor pad in Gloucester Road it was not long before he and Hattie were living together – rather daring for that period. John and June's divorce came through in 1947 and Mum and Dad married two years later at Kensington Register Office.

'Would you mind awfully if we got hitched?'

My brother, Kim, was born on 12th October 1956. I vaguely remember thinking, 'what's this invading the household?' but soon came to realise he was part of my eventual amazing but dysfunctional family. I remember Mum breastfeeding my brother Kim and wondering what on earth was going on…

He was named after the Rudyard Kipling book and character, but when he was old enough, while at school, he took the name 'Jake' as he hated the name Kim. I don't really know for sure but I think he chose Jake as a homage to Jacques, my mother's maiden name. From here on, I'll refer to him as Jake which I'm sure he would appreciate. We became very close growing up although we were quite different. Jake was cheeky and far more mischievous than I was. I remember, one firework night, asking strangers for money to buy some bangers and rockets. I was pushing him around in his pram outside Earl's Court tube station. He was made up like a Guy Fawkes 'guy' and he suddenly erupted out of the pram brandishing a cup for donations! Older ladies, completely astonished, screamed but eventually calmed down, and told us we were very naughty boys – but still gave us a copper or two. We loved 5th November. I was much more like my dad, a little reserved, whereas Jake was more outgoing and much more like Mum. We were very distinct characters, but not at all competitive – even later when we were both pursuing musical careers.

Mum was already making her mark outside the Players' in the radio series of *ITMA* and in films. She was soon back at work after my birth and Dad was in demand too and so there was a constant supply of Spanish and German au pairs to look after Jake and me. I know that in later life, Mum and Dad regretted how little time they saw of us when Jake and I were very small, but they obviously couldn't turn down work.

There was also assistance of a 'mother's help' in the unlikely form of gay actor John Bailey – a friend of Mum and Dad's. John Bailey was a graduate of the Rank Organisation's 'Charm School', an institution for young film actors, but had lost his contract when he was discovered to be gay, which was still illegal in those unenlightened times. He was arrested when an Italian lover tried to enter the UK and had been sentenced to three years in jail for 'importuning an alien for immoral purposes'. He naturally found it very difficult to get acting work on his release from prison and actually survived by making curtains.

Neither of my parents had any concerns about having him look after us. Mum was completely without any prejudicial feelings when it came to gay men so that 'a friend of Hattie's' took on exactly the same connotation as 'a friend of Dorothy's'. This outlook stemmed from the time when Mum lived in Chelsea shortly after my grandfather was killed. It was a very liberal part of the capital to live in during the 1920s and had attracted a bohemian community of writers, artists and intellectuals since the beginning of the century.

According to Bruce Copp, later to become my Godfather and a celebrated theatrical restaurateur, Mum, from a very early age, and certainly during her formative years, was 'quite used to seeing the parade of flamboyant characters that frequented her neighbourhood and men in drag who attended the annual Chelsea Arts Ball'. In fact, in later years, she surrounded herself with a coterie of gay men and always maintained that this period in her life paved the way for her absolute acceptance of homosexuals.

In fact one of my earliest memories was at the age of two and being in the care of John Bailey. I was sitting in a high chair, refusing to eat my carrots. I hated carrots. To this day, I don't mind a raw carrot, but a tepid cooked carrot is completely unappealing. I just wouldn't budge, but the problem was John Bailey wouldn't give in either. I've found that actors can be pretty stubborn and he just wouldn't let me out of the chair until I ate them. We were both pretty obdurate and I sat there for what seemed like hours before I gave in and ate the horrible things.

John Bailey had a friend, Willie Preston, who had a farm in Northants, which he shared with his wife, Natalie and two children. A few years later John used to take us up there to stay. It was a great place for a couple of urban boys to play. There were forty acres to explore, haystacks to mess about in and fresh eggs to collect and devour. It was all very different from Earl's Court. The family also had a dog called Peg – a Jack Russell who had lost her leg in a tractor accident, but used to race around on her remaining three legs.

Our house was lovely. A real home. Warm in character and atmosphere, but physically cold in the winter. There was no central heating, but that was normal in a Victorian house in those days. The only heating we had was the fireplace in the basement where we spent most of our time. When we were young, I remember my brother and I being bathed in a zinc tub in front of the fire. 'Demons', was how Dad described the red burning embers at the base of the chimney. I don't know why but it always made me laugh. And I remember that the drain would always back up on the concrete just outside the kitchen and Dad would be there trying to clear it. That was the only time I ever saw him doing anything remotely close to keeping the house safe. It was my responsibility, at a very early age, to fix the fuses when they blew.

The family spent most of our time in the basement of the house where the living room, my bedroom and the kitchen was situated, though Mum and Dad, to begin with, slept in the first floor front room. And to top things off we had to use the outside toilet from time to time.

All I need is a Strat

And in the winter… well you can imagine. I don't want to sound like a character from a Monty Python sketch but that's the way it was. I was very excited when the coal men used to deliver – it always seemed like a day to celebrate. I can still hear the sound of the men opening the manhole and dumping the coal into the cellar, dust and all.

Just by the basement door there was a rack for overcoats. Being inquisitive and for no reason I can remember, I set fire to one of the coats hanging there. At first it started to smoulder and proceeded to catch fire. I slowly walked back to the living room and told Mum and Dad there was a fire by the door. I think initially they didn't believe me but I persuaded them to take a look. It wasn't too bad but they had to douse the flames, pretty sharpish. Mum asked me how it started. I remember telling her that when they make the coats they put fire in the lining and sometimes it gets out! I wasn't scolded, and I think at the time she must have believed me. What some kids can get away with. Especially us – I think we were indulged because Mum and Dad felt a bit guilty about being away working so much and so when we were all together they did let us get away with a lot!

Apart from the coal men, there were also deliveries from the milkman; he had a horse and cart and the horse would always stop at exactly the right house for the deliveries of milk, eggs and whatnot. The funny thing being, that he and the horse would stop about five houses down from us for about half an hour, once a week when the bill was due. Perhaps the housewife who lived there kept a bale of hay for the horse. Well, something like that anyway. Then there was the rag and bone man, who came around once a week. A real life 'Steptoe'. A very nice bloke with nothing more than a cart full of rubbish really. We hardly had anything to give him. (Sorry, if you're still alive and reading this!)

And then there were the gypsies, trying to sell us lavender and if we refused, a curse was put upon the entire house, which went unheeded. I recall the onion salesmen, who rode bicycles selling onions and garlic. Proper French blokes with striped shirts and berets! Mum would always buy their wares. I believe they used to take the ferry from France and then a train up to London. How on earth they made a profit I have no idea, but they called around on a regular basis during the summer months.

All the years I lived at home, it always seemed like an on-going party. Mum and Dad constantly had friends over. Some famous people 'in the business', some not so famous, and it just seemed never ending. Having said that, later on in my life Mum admitted to me that she always needed to summon up the courage to enter the living room, even with very close friends because of her weight problem which she had been fighting for as long as I can remember. Recalling this makes me a little sad, but what bravado she had! Plus, another amazing trick she could always perform was being able to feed what seemed like an army with two eggs and a little bread. How she did that still confounds me to this day.

I remember in those early days there were still signs of what England endured during the Second World War. There were so many bomb sites all over London and its environs. And prefab houses everywhere – 'temporary' single storey buildings erected immediately after the war to house bombed out families. I think some still exist over seventy years later!

It was difficult to comprehend exactly what went on and how those heroic people managed to cope with it all. I guess that's the English for you… stubborn, resilient and unyielding. I remember my dad telling us during the Blitz, he was going out to a show in the West End one night and when he got back the house in which he resided, it had disappeared – completely destroyed! I remember asking a lot of questions about the war and what Mum and Dad did during that terrible period. Mum was a nurse for some of the war, but was also a welder in a factory making Bailey Bridges and would lead her fellow workers in renditions of music hall songs! When Dad was conscripted he was told, 'Well, you'll never make a soldier, so we'll send you off to officers training camp'. He actually became a tank commander in India! What???

I have to tell a funny story about my dad in India. He was coerced to going to a house of ill repute by a colleague – something that he wasn't really ready for. But nevertheless he went. The address was Number 4 Grant Rd. Bombay. Of course, being him, nothing occurred apart from the 'hostess' simply asking for a pen to write to her family. Of course he obliged and gave her one (a pen)… Years later, he was doing a TV show in Bristol, a kind of general knowledge quiz, and was asked, 'If all the good girls go to heaven, where do the bad girls go?' To which he replied, 'Number 4 Grant Rd. Bombay.' There was huge laugh from someone in the audience, who obviously knew the address from being in the army. My dad had the driest sense of humor I have ever known.

'Stumps' in Margate

2

'LEAD ME TO THE ROCK'

Hattie Jacques
67 Eardley Crescent SW5

Dear Johnny

Thank you for telling me your news, I do feel I would like to tell you that truly and sincerely I wish for your happiness, for your peace of mind and for everything to be good in your future marriage. Joan is a lovely person and loves you and is much better for you than I could ever have been. We have all been through a pretty wretched time but out of it all I'm sure will come great happiness for all of us.

God bless and my love.
Jo

For the most part I hated school… and for the other part too. Ugh! The first place I attended was a kind of pre-school, where we spent much time carving salt blocks (why???), painting, afternoon naps, learning basic alphabet etc. etc. I used to walk there as it was not far from home. I remember the staff being nice but that's about it.

My second school was a prep school in Cadogan Square London called Sussex House, a very posh feeder school to Eton, which had a strong reputation for music and drama and where the motto was, somewhat ironically, '*Lead me to the rock that is higher than I*' – although the governors were probably thinking of the rock that had nothing to do with Hendrix or The Stones. I felt completely out of place. I was so into music by that time that anything they tried to teach me went in one ear and out the other. I used to ride there and back on my bike except when we used to have those terrible smog days called 'peasoupers'. You really could only see about five feet in front of you!

There was one thing that helped me get through those days; the school choir. We had quite a good music teacher, his name was Mr Hunt. He encouraged me to join the choir which was a way of getting away for trips to sing in some of the most beautiful cathedrals in England. A day away from lessons and a chance to travel. When I read Keith Richards' book *Life*, I discovered that apparently he had a similar idea and joined his school choir for the same reasons. Funnily enough, he is the only other person I know that has a name for each of his guitars as I do! I'll introduce you to them later.

I don't suppose I had a name for my first guitar which was given to me when I was nine years old. It was a gift from Spain from Peter Greenwell, composer and pianist, who had been Hattie's accompanist before working in the same capacity with Noel Coward. Before that my instrument was a plastic ukulele which unlike, George Formby, I didn't get lots more pleasure from playing (funnily enough a ukulele was also Hendrix's first ever instrument).

I took to my new guitar immediately – I never had any lessons and found that I had a natural feeling for the instrument. The guitar became my life. Even at that early age I knew that was my future. I began to listen to all the music that affected me. We had a '78' record player at home and would go through all the discs my parents had. Mostly jazz. There was one that I found by Louis Armstrong called 'St James' Infirmary', it was really blues based rather than jazz but it hit a nerve with me. I think I wore it out, or at least dozens of needles. I also listened to Lena Horne, Billie Holliday, and Ella Fitzgerald.

Then Rock 'n' Roll came into my life. I was hooked. By this time I was thirteen or so and loved what I was hearing, and tried to emulate the guitar playing of these great artists. All I wanted to do was be a part of it all. All the way from pop music to blues… mostly English groups, Stones, Beatles, Shadows, but also American blues artists such as Muddy Waters, Robert Johnson, Sonny Boy Williamson, John Lee Hooker. Then came Jimi Hendrix, Cream, and Fleetwood Mac with the fabulous Peter Green, Jeremy Spencer and Danny Kirwain – all great guitarists.

I played for the first time in front of an audience at the age of twelve at a secondary school concert. Unfortunately Westminster City Grammar school wasn't much more successful or happier for me than Sussex House. It was structured like a public school, as are a number of long-established grammar schools. The building was in neo-gothic style and pretty imposing. Most of the teachers wore gowns and there were very few female teachers so it was all pretty daunting for a twelve-year-old. There were strict uniform rules (including the wearing of a cap) and we had to wear a white or grey shirt. A contemporary of mine, Robin Gray recalled, 'We got our mums to convert narrow school ties to kipper ties – anything to look cool'.

Because I had famous parents who were on the television, radio and films, I was constantly picked on. In fact I was bullied regularly. And like the victims of bullying, none of it was my doing. Surprisingly, having a celebrity mother and father was the cause of harassment. My 'schoolmates' – and I use the term loosely – assumed that having famous parents, who appeared regularly on television, meant that we were very wealthy and consequently I was given a hard time. We were certainly comfortably off but not nearly as wealthy as some of the other pupils assumed. Actually, in those days, the BBC paid very a minimal sum for their work. Once, on a morning break, I was stabbed in my lower back with a pair of compasses. That wasn't pleasant. Thinking back, it might have been pretty serious if they had punctured my spine. I had and still have no idea who did it. Bastard, whoever it was!

There were other forms of torture – the usual forcing of heads down toilets. Towel-flicking in changing rooms. Elastic bands on six-inch rulers aimed for the crotch. Robin Gray remembers, 'Boys standing behind you in morning assembly would hit you in the back of the knees to make you fall. Short trousers in the first year would be a big mistake. The secondary modern school, Buckingham Gate, down the road could be a source of attacks from time to time after school'.

And, to be honest, I had difficulty with the academic side of schooling too. The only subjects that interested me were history, geography and a few aspects of physics – everything else was such a bore. Maths and algebra were completely unintelligible to me (In recent years I've actually become very interested in physics and I am a huge fan of the American/ Japanese academic and theoretical physicist, Michio Kaku, a genius indeed).

The maths teacher also taught Music and he seemed to be pre-occupied with 'Hear My Prayer' – the Christian anthem and particularly the passage known as, 'O for the Wings of a Dove'. During the music period upon which he targeted his personal taste and which seemed very limited to me, we were asked to bring in a recording of our choice for the next lesson. 'Great,' I thought. 'I can't wait to bring something I love!' So, the next week came around and I happily brought in a Muddy Waters LP. Eventually it was my turn to play a track from the album. He asked me which song to play to which I replied, 'Any one of them.' I think he just placed the stylus on the first track, can't remember what song it was but was most likely 'King Bee'.

He listened to it for about thirty seconds, lifted the needle, looked at me and barked, 'That's not music, it's rubbish!' I stood up and said, 'Sir, I beg to differ.' Without a moment's hesitation he told me to report to the headmaster's study immediately for being disrespectful. What?!?!

Anyway I made my way down the corridor and rapped on his door awaiting the order 'Come' from inside, which was always used at that time. I walked in, told him why I was there. He rolled his eyes and told me to wait for my next class. Later on that year there was a parent-teacher evening which Dad attended. He was asked to talk to several teachers and, yes, you've guessed it, one being the maths/music teacher. He proceeded to tell Dad that my maths was terrible and I had awful taste in music! With typical understatement, Dad replied, 'Oh I see. Well, as it happens, I only got two percent in my last mathematics test. And actually, do you know, my son's taste in music is hugely Catholic!' (Just in case, Catholic in that sense means broad.) I was so happy my fabulous dad stuck up for me. I don't think there was much more discussion between them.

I wasn't much more at home on the sports field. I was also forced to play football and rugby and those days always seemed to be the coldest days of the year. The south London sports fields were also mainly waterlogged and we always got covered in mud and soaked through. I once played centre-forward in the school team. When the sports teacher, Mr Wooley, blew the whistle to start then game, I scored from the kick off, but apparently that's not allowed and so the goal was disallowed. If I knew anything about football I would probably have felt as a sick as a parrot.

I went to the head teacher Mr Alder and told him, 'I'm afraid football isn't my thing.' He asked me what else I could do, which floored me before he suggested, 'What about rowing on the Thames?' I agreed as this seemed a bit more of an interesting proposition and so I rowed in an eight for the school for two years and funnily enough, I quite enjoyed messing about on the river, although I hated getting my feet wet. My school friend Richard McNeff reminded me that Mr Alder used to move a large oar that he had hanging on his study wall and would remove it and carry it around somewhat threateningly if any of us was sent to see him. There was one teacher so frail and thin that he was rumoured to have a tape worm – although no-one really knew what that meant. Another, during lessons, would unconsciously remove his shoe and strap his wristwatch to his ankle. This, of course, led to constant requests from pupils innocently asking for the time, leading to him having to peer down at his foot for the correct answer.

Oh, and then there was 'Chalky White' who took great pleasure in checking the length of everybody's hair before assembly in the morning. I thought it was ridiculous at the time. Naturally beards were also forbidden. One of the guys managed to grow some whiskers (more than I could do then) but made sure it didn't meet at the chin. Chalky was bemused when he was told they were sideburns and not a beard and so technically allowed. I can't remember what he taught but he was definitely a piece of work. In fact he loved to enforce all the school rules. He didn't have much charisma and was pretty stern most of the time and impossible to argue with. He actually got his wish and later became Headmaster when Mr Alder left.

Robin Gray also recalled that he once tried to play my guitar before a concert or a play. (That's ok, Robin – glad you finally 'fessed up) and he made 'a lot of noise'. A teacher came in to protest – not for the first time that someone has complained about the sound coming from my guitar! The English department used to produce some excellent school plays and I remember being 'press ganged' into one. And I use the phrase wisely because I had no interest in acting at all. The play was *The Caucasian Chalk Circle*. I would have much preferred to be working backstage – such as lighting or props but not performing and having to remember lines.

After I left they produced a play about WW1, written by pupils and based on contemporary letters and school magazines. This would have interested me because an ancestor of mine called Haviland Le Mesurier was a captain in the Great War and kept diaries and wrote many letters back to England from the trenches. In fact the diaries and letters were published a few years ago and were written and produced for a one man play that my stepmother Joannie and I went to see in London. It was very good and quite moving to know that the actor was playing a family member. Sadly, he was killed in action.

I suppose it was only natural with both parents who were actors that I would have a go at acting and I auditioned for a part in *The Horse without a Head*, an episode of the Walt Disney Television series entitled *The Wonderful World of Color*. The programme aired in October 1963 and was about a group of French slum children who share only one toy – a headless wooden horse on wheels. The kids foil a robbery when a thief stashes the key to his hiding place inside the horse. I did ok at the audition, repeated my lines correctly but I was far more interested in the technology and what went on behind the camera and so didn't get the part. Acting was never for me and so I've been 'resting' ever since.

It was around this period at Westminster City that I became friends with a couple of guys there. My closest friend was the aforementioned Richard McNeff. Strangely enough, his birthday is two days after mine. We both had the same interests in life and used to go to the nearest pub for a pint at lunchtime. I assume we looked old enough to drink then as we were never refused.

Richard, a teacher and author, is now living in London and I'm still in contact with him, although we weren't in touch for a while. We shared a common bond in that his dad was also an actor and so his background was a little similar to mine and he understood that way of life. His dad, also called Richard, had made a number of stage and television appearances and was known among *Dr Who* fans for having been 'exterminated' by the Daleks in on one of the early series. He had actually dropped William Hartnell, the first Doctor, while having to carry him on set, which didn't amuse the 'Time Lord' very much!

Our friendship coincided with those difficult adolescent years, which existed to the backdrop of hippiedom. It was as Richard described, 'As if we had been living in a black and white film and then suddenly the images were transformed into vivid technicolour'. We shared a love of music and Richard actually helped with the lighting for a school band with which I was involved. There was one disastrous gig at The American School when the oils used for the psychedelic lighting effects spilled all over the concert room floor.

I recall visiting Richard in Brighton when he was studying at Sussex University and telling him I was going to appear on television in the Eurovision Song Contest. He was very impressed until I told him it was with The Wombles!

We didn't see each other for some years until I was on a European tour with Rod Stewart. We were just about to land in our private plane at San Sebastián, in the Basque country, in the north west of Spain. For some reason I was thinking about Richard, wondering what he was up to and how he was doing – I don't know why I thought of him as I hadn't seen him for years.

We got to our hotel, and as we were checking in, one of the clerks gave me an envelope addressed to me. I was thinking, 'who the fuck knows me here?' Turned out it was Richard! How weird was that? He had lived a rather nomadic life in Spain teaching English as a foreign language and had hung out with Ronnie Wood (Stones) and Roger Taylor (Queen). He was now living in the Basque country. So, we met up, caught up and had a fabulous couple of days reminiscing, eating tapas and of course drinking copious amounts of alcohol.

There was also another incredible coincidence: the week before I arrived he had been in a record shop, had picked up a Rod Stewart record and discovered that I had co-written a song called 'Sweet Surrender' only to find the band were in town that weekend. He came to the show, hung out backstage and even went on the tour bus where he recalled Rod wrapping himself in an enormous tartan blanket!

I'm afraid neither Mum nor Dad was very helpful when it came to academic aspirations. Dad later wrote, 'Some parents are very good at helping their children with their homework but Hattie and I failed miserably, as neither of us could add up or do simple subtraction, let alone cope with the mysteries of Latin algebra or chemistry… so what the boys learned from us were things like what was right and wrong and hopefully how to say "please" and "thank you".' My dad always believed that good manners and a certain amount of charm can take anyone anywhere they fancy and despite my rock and roll lifestyle, I have tried to follow this ethos.

Apart from schooldays which were clearly not the happiest days of my life, my childhood memories were otherwise extremely pleasurable. Mum was a devoted, loving mother and Dad would play cricket with Jake and me on Barnes Common… usually with one hand in his pocket and a cigarette in his mouth. On Saturday mornings I used to go with Dad to a record 'emporium' near South Kensington underground station where we would search for rare jazz 78s. Dad took me to the Bull's Head at Barnes, which was a famous jazz haunt and also to the legendary jazz club, Ronnie Scott's in Soho, where I met a number of celebrated musicians including pianist, Oscar Peterson. A charming giant of a man. I can still picture his big beautiful smile. The musicians were so accessible and we met so many world famous artistes.

Dad was very friendly with Ronnie, who always greeted him warmly at the club. Apart from being an excellent tenor saxophonist, Ronnie was famous for his stand up routine at the beginning of the set – with oft repeated jokes. He was always amusing about the club itself, 'It's just like home – filthy and full of strangers. I hope you enjoyed the food – a thousand flies can't be wrong. It was very quiet last night. We had the bouncers chucking people IN. I've played with lots of bassists… and he's one of them. Our vocalist is so shy, she eats a banana sideways.' Etc etc. Lovely.

There were also several trips to the circus which rekindled Dad's childhood fascination with the 'Big Top' although Jake and I were never impressed. Dad adored the circus and insisted on taking us at every opportunity. I think he especially liked all the pageantry and rituals and particularly the parade around the ring, which in those days included elephants and lions. It was something that I never really got. I never saw what he saw in it. And to this day, clowns really irritate me! In fact years later, I was offered the opportunity to join Cockney Rebel, but my hatred of clowns prevented me from joining them as I would have had to have donned a red nose, baggy trousers and face paint.

Life at 67 Eardley Crescent was definitely great fun, but it was also somewhat chaotic. I used to share a room with Jake and I remember being woken up regularly in the middle of the night by the likes of Peter Sellers, Spike Milligan, Michael Bentine and various jazz musicians jamming loudly somewhere in the house. To this day I'm asked frequently what it was like growing up in such a bohemian household, but it didn't seem out of the ordinary. To me, Kenneth Williams, Joan Sims and Harry Secombe were just friends and colleagues of Mum and Dad's. It was the 1960s and so there was inevitably a lot of popping of pills and smoking dope, but incredible as it sounds, to me, this was just normal. Some of them were more than a little fond of a little hash – and I'm not talking the corned beef dish. In fact, years later, Mum told me she found some in a drawer that must have been forgotten about. She could have given it to me! My childhood was certainly 'charmed' and I would never have swapped this lifestyle for a more traditional upbringing.

There were so many stories from my wonderful but dysfunctional family. Everything from my early years seemed to me to be calm, full of peace and enjoyable. The people that came and went to my home were interesting, odd sometimes, but nearly all fascinating and certainly eccentric. I remember one lady, whose name was Mary Ogg. She was always dressed in what seemed to be Victorian clothes. Apparently she was an actress that Mum and Dad knew and felt some sort of responsibility towards her. To this day I don't know why. She was sweet enough and was kind to me and Jake. But every time she went out, she always helped herself to five shillings or so from a jar that was left on the dresser. I was told she lost her husband some years previously in a tragic accident. Apparently, they were both on a train, he opened the window to get some air and was decapitated as the train entered a tunnel. I can't imagine the scene. Anyway, she was a fixture for some time at home. And then she vanished. I suppose she died, because I never saw her again.

Dad had a lot of friends, but was also very close to Mum's brother, Robin, who I was named after – as well as my grandfather. He was an extremely handsome and dapper man and who, in later years, became a prolific illustrator for the *Radio Times, Punch* and *The Listener* and over one hundred novels. He was perhaps best known for his illustrations of the *Hornblower* books by C. S. Forrester. My uncle Robin was probably one of the last distinguished illustrators never to have had any formal training. Dad used to spend a lot of time with Robin, doing the rounds of Soho clubs but usually ending up at Ronnie Scott's.

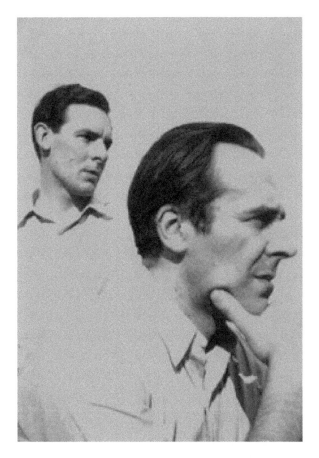

Uncle Robin and Dad – in search of a jazz club (JOHN PAUL JACQUES)

Mum was very funny at home. She wasn't slapstick, comedic funny but she was dry funny. Her temperament was outgoing and loving. It was impossible for her to go anywhere without being recognised but she never turned down requests for an autograph or a photograph and she'd use her popularity to help charities. She was, in fact, a tireless charity worker, but never made a big deal of it or courted publicity.

When I was a small boy she took me along to a police charity function. At the end of the evening they presented her with a special pair of handcuffs as a gift. The next morning I got hold of them and locked myself up. It was a bit of a joke at first until we realised we couldn't get them off. When she carted me down the street to the nearest police station I yelled at passersby, 'I haven't done anything, missus, please don't lock me up!' I thought it was very funny, although not sure Mum did. And when we did finally get to the police station they didn't have a key to undo the cuffs so she had to take me to a locksmith. It wasn't a total disaster because later, when Mum was working with Eric Sykes in their celebrated television series, Sykes wrote a whole episode based on that incident.

I adored my grandmother Mary, who was, by now, living in Margate in a lovely, old stone six bedroom cottage that Mum had bought for her. It was in a beautiful position with spectacular views of the sea. Both Jake and I would be packed off there for holidays whilst Mum and Dad were working. The seaside house was a popular stopping off place for family and friends – a sort of Eardley Crescent by the sea. Mary was an amazing character, who used to tell us that the cottage was owned by an old fisherman and that there was stolen treasure somewhere in the house! She was very sweet and her kindness and sociability was of great influence on Mum and the way she lived her life. There's actually a blue plaque on the house at 25 Trinity Square, Margate which incorrectly states that John Le Mesurier and Hattie Jacques lived here.

Mum also loved to entertain and her generosity of spirit rubbed off on all her friends and family. She was definitely the home maker while my dad was not the most domesticated of men. Even the act of making a cup of tea seemed to be beyond his practical capabilities and confused him no end. I do have to say, however, that his persona of being helpless and otherworldly was sometimes utilised to get out of any simple household task. He was certainly a professional in this respect. In fact he should have got a BAFTA for portraying vague.

I grew up in a very gentle household where there was never a cross word. Mum and Dad really loved each other and although they both had affairs, everyone thought that they would always stay together. That all changed, however, when I was about eight years old. I remember, one day, a very dashing, good looking man coming to the house. His

Wake up and smell the honeysuckle. Mum and my Grandmother Mary in Margate.

name was John Schofield and was initially employed to drive Mum to work and charity events. Mum was involved deeply with the Leukemia Research Fund as was John, who had lost a son to that awful disease. Both Jake and I immediately latched on to him. He was funny, charming and a different kind of man from whom we were used to. And all the time we had no idea what was really going on between him and Mum.

At first, Dad, who was the most diffident and easy going man you could meet, was unaware of the affair but even he couldn't fail to notice something was amiss when Schofield actually moved into their house and Dad ended up occupying a bed-sit on the top floor! But, amazingly, there didn't seem to be any animosity whatsoever between them. Life seemed quite normal, and went on as if nothing had changed in the household.

But one day I happened to read in a newspaper that Mum and Dad were getting a divorce. It was the first I knew about it. I told Jake and then I remember tearing the article up. I just didn't want to believe what we were reading. We were both shocked, but didn't really understand why this was happening as there was no fighting between Mum and Dad. Life seemed to be quite normal. Normal? Ha! Nothing was really 'normal' at Eardley Crescent. In the end, Dad actually took the responsibility as co-respondent so Mum wouldn't get the flack and possibly hurt her career.

The thing is that Jake and I loved John Schofield and we became very close to him. He was a very charismatic, funny and charming bloke – a cross between Cary Grant and George Clooney. It was as if I had two families... it was almost like a bonus at the time – although of course we were very young and pre-occupied with our own lives. It didn't seem confusing at all. He was another father figure – and quite different to the way Dad played his role. Complicated I know, but that's how it was. Dad was working an awful lot at that time – so he was often out of the house, but when he was around, he was the quiet reserved one whereas John Schofield had a very gregarious and outgoing personality. The house was always busy and hectic, full of visitors, friends and guests and so having Schofield living with us wasn't that unusual. Dad was not someone to let on how he felt. At the time, I didn't really feel sorry for him because he never showed any sadness. He wasn't angry, but then he just wasn't into confrontation – much like me.

Four generations in a very awkward 'This is Your Life'.

During Mum's affair with him, in February 1963 mum was 'tricked' into appearing on the popular television programme, *This is Your Life*, hosted by Eamon Andrews. She really had no idea about the show and had been rehearsing with Eric Sykes at the BBC when Eamonn Andrews appeared from behind a newspaper he had been hiding behind. I thought she was really quite brave about the whole thing and put on her 'Hattie' persona beautifully. I have a copy of the show, and when Dad came on and spoke about Mum he said something like, 'The way she looks after the household and the children is really quite a clever trick.' He was obviously referring to our situation at home with John Schofield being there. The studio audience and viewing public had no idea that she and Dad were in the middle of a marital crisis. It was all incredibly awkward, but somehow – as in real life – they carried it off. Jake and I came on at the end with my grandmother and great grandmother.

Despite the difficult circumstances, Dad seemed content to continue in this manner. I don't whether it was his deep love for Mum and not wanting to let her go or simply inertia. In fact, I don't think he would have ever moved out of the family home without Mum prompting his departure – for the best possible reasons. Seeing her future with John, but so concerned for Dad's happiness, she set about trying to find him a new wife. She introduced Dad to Joan Malin who worked at The Establishment club in Soho, London, which was a big hangout for actors and musicians. Strangely enough Bruce Copp ran the restaurant there.

I first met my future stepmother Joan when I was about ten years old. There was an inevitable party at Eardley Crescent and Jake and I stayed up wanting to join in. Dad asked Joan if she wanted to meet us and I remember we were sitting up in our beds when they came in. I'd just been given a bicycle for my birthday and Jake said to Joan, 'How would you feel if your brother had got a bike and wouldn't let you share it?' Joan said she'd feel very jealous which didn't help me much in my attempts to keep my bike away from my brother. To deflect her, I asked what she did. Joannie replied, 'I'm a private detective and I also write ghost stories under an assumed name.' An answer that immediately intrigued both of us, but which turned out to be nonsense – although her response perfectly demonstrated her sense of fun. I got on with Joan right from the start. She was… and is great – the absolute opposite of the wicked stepmother, although I sometimes like to refer to her as this sort of Disney character. Joan also got on fantastically well with my mum, which made things so much easier. Jake also became very good friends with Joan's son David.

All of a sudden, Jake and I had two sets of parents, all four of whom we loved deeply. Dad and Joan (I now call her Joannie) took a flat in Barons Court which was only two stops away on the tube from Earl's Court and so very close to us. We would go there two or three times a week to spend time with them, and come home in the evening to Eardley Crescent. We also went on holidays together. Once on a trip to Paris, Jake shat his pants halfway up the Eiffel Tower and we had to abandon his pants somewhere in the iconic structure. Years later I returned to the area around the Eiffel tower to play concerts with Johnny Hallyday and both times I wondered if his pants were hidden somewhere in the tower.

In time it was mutually agreed that Mum initiate divorce

proceedings so that Dad and Joannie could marry. Joannie was still married but separated from her actor husband, Mark Eden at the time and was named as co-respondent. In actual fact, a 'double divorce' was obtained on the same day in May 1965. Joannie was given a decree nisi on the grounds of desertion, but in Mum and Dad's divorce it was Dad who was declared the adulterer rather than Mum in order to protect her career. Mum's relationship with John Schofield was also kept secret so as not to harm her reputation and it was thus decided that the best way to handle the media was to admit Joan's affair with Dad thereby casting Mum in the role of victim and poor Joannie was branded a marriage breaker by the press. She wasn't entirely happy about this, but played her part like a proper trouper. She later wrote, 'I was the younger woman who had wrecked Hattie's marriage, so we couldn't smile or acknowledge each other but as she left the courtroom staring straight ahead, she blew me a kiss.'

Dad gave Jake and me a penknife each, feeling a little guilty. After the divorce Mum was quoted in the press, 'John was and still is a gentle and very lovely man. We are still great friends… it doesn't matter how civilised people are about dissolving a marriage; it's still a wretched business. John and I are the greatest friends and still I love him and I think he loves me. There were never any recriminations. I wouldn't have been able to stand that, bad feelings between the parents of children. He's a lovely person, so sweet…' That was all so true.

When Dad and Joannie decided to marry, we wrote to congratulate them:

Dear Daddy and Joan,
I hope you have a happy marriage, it's a lovely idea.
I love you both a lot. Kim

Dear Daddy and Joan
I am really glad that you are getting married, because I love you very much. I hope you are very happy together, I know Kim and I will like it a lot.
All my love, Robin

Dad and Joannie married at Fulham Town Hall on 2nd March 1966 and dear old Bruce Copp was best man. Jake and I sent them a drawing of two goldfish representing us, swimming around in a bowl with two smaller fish with their names on them and heart shaped bubbles.

3

MUSIC, MUSIC, MUSIC

Anything seemed possible in 1966. There was a search for new forms of expression, the 'counter culture' was a phrase that tripped off the tongue – that is if you weren't too stoned. Radical politics were to the fore as was experimental film and audacious fashion. England even won the World Cup. London was the capital of cool and certainly swinging. And in terms of music, LPs outsold singles for the first time and pirate radio stations were at their zenith. And me? I was exploiting the music scene... well... sort of.

When I was about thirteen or fourteen, 'mobile discos' were very popular for parties, weddings and lots of office Christmas bashes. So borrowing the cash I needed from mum, I built one. It was very rudimentary; two turntables, a tiny mixer, an amplifier and a one speaker cabinet plus some headphones to line up the next song. I used to 'cold call' all the record labels I could and managed to get them to send me what were called 'advance copies'.

The companies were more than happy to help as it was free promotion for them. So, almost every other weekend, I would be out 'working' the parties. It was great fun – like getting paid to play! I was once employed at a wedding reception in the East End. My playlist wasn't going down well and a bloke came up to me and asked, 'Do you know the 'Hokey Cokey?', 'No,' I replied somewhat perfunctorily. That didn't seem to go down very well. 'Well, I've just come out the nick for GBH, so you'd better find something more suitable than the crap you're playing.' For some reason I didn't have any version of the 'Hokey Cokey', but I must have found something to keep him happy because I still have my knees.

I was also lucky because at this time John Schofield decided to become a promoter, and he had a regular venue in Hastings at the pier ballroom. He booked all sorts of rock and roll acts during the summer of '66. Better yet, I got to be the DJ there, again playing what was current at the time and so I was able to see bands such as Pink Floyd, Amen Corner, Status Quo and The Move among many others. During this time I discovered 'the blues' and spent much time learning the craft of players like John Lee Hooker, Muddy Waters, Eric Clapton, Jimi Hendrix and Jeff Beck.

John used to drive me down to Hastings in the company of his 'secretary', Linda Kattan, who helped him while he was promoting the pier ballroom shows. I later discovered she was having an affair with him while he was with Mum. But that's another story. In any case, she used to work for Radio London, the pirate radio station, before the BBC managed to close down all the offshore stations. One of the DJs there was a very nice guy called Pete Drummond. He used to 'MC' the shows in Hastings before working as one of the earliest presenters on for BBC Radio 1 just before John Peel. Anyway, I latched onto him and we became quite friendly. Some years later, I was in London picking up a work permit for the US and bumped into Pete in Kilburn. It was great to see him again and we lunched in a local Indian restaurant. He was just as charming and funny as I remembered him to be and if I recall correctly, he was wearing the same three quarter length black PVC macintosh he used to wear when I first met him.

Although there is no doubt that John Schofield was genuinely fond of Mum there was a feeling among some of mum's friends that he was just using her for her fame and her incredibly generous nature. John used his East End charm to devastating effect and once in mum's inner circle, attempted to seduce a number of her friends and acquaintances. Mum couldn't have been oblivious to this and must have known there was some truth to her friends' accusations, but, in any case she remained devoted to him… and, of course, I was much too young to be aware about what was going on.

I believe that, on the whole, John treated Mum well, but there were a couple of worrying occasions when both Bruce and Dad had evidence of John hitting Mum. There was no excuse for this and it's possible that he might have lost his temper when mum confronted him about his lascivious behaviour. My mum suffered constantly from lack of self esteem due to her weight and could never quite believe that John had fallen for her.

In the middle of 1966, Mum travelled to Rome to appear in *The Bobo*, which featured Peter Sellers and Britt Ekland. The movie was shot at Cinecitta in Rome, probably the most famous studio in Italy. I visited the set on a couple of occasions when I stayed for a long weekend. I knew Peter Sellers, who was a regular visitor to Eardley Crescent, but I had never met Britt Ekland and as a pre-pubescent teenager immediately developed a serious crush on her before falling in love with her. And who could blame me? Funnily enough, years later when I was tuning guitars for Rod Stewart the band all went out for dinner and Britt was then in a relationship with Rod. He went to introduce me, but before he could complete the niceties, she interrupted, 'Oh, I know Robin. I met him years ago.' I like to think she had never forgotten me...

Mum loved working on the film and described it as one of the loveliest things she'd worked on – although she was hiding the truth. Before filming started, she went on the biggest diet she'd ever taken and lost five stone. This may have been a vain attempt to keep John because he visited her on location and told her that he had met an Italian heiress with whom he had fallen in love.

At the end of filming, Mum returned home but was hospitalised soon after for investigations about a kidney complaint. Some years later, she told me that John had visited her in hospital and told her he was ending the relationship. He threw a medallion on the bed that she had given him (three fingers moulded together in gold and inscribed 'I Love You') and stormed out. I was surprised when I first heard this as I didn't think it was in his nature to behave in such a rude and insensitive manner, but it made me very angry. I suppose John must have felt so guilty and upset about what he had done to Mum that the only way he could cope with it himself was to be so brutally frank. What was even stranger was that he literally disappeared out of our lives. He didn't return to Eardley Crescent to collect his belongings and didn't say goodbye to Jake or me.

Although she mainly kept it from us – she was never really one to express her feelings that much – she did confide in her closest friends and was clearly heartbroken. Bruce felt that she was never quite the same again and her weight ballooned. Joannie always said that Mum lost some of her sparkle, 'It was as if one of the lights that made her so iridescent had gone out, like one or two lights in a chandelier. Things looked the same but slightly dimmer.' I was therefore a bit taken aback when Mum later told me that, after the split, she and John used to meet for the odd clandestine rendezvous!

Sadly things were not going well for Dad and Joannie. She had fallen in love with comedian Tony Hancock and continued a volatile affair which only came to an end with the comedian's tragic overdose in Australia in 1968. Again, I didn't really know what was going on at the time. Jake and I used to go to Barons Court to visit Dad a couple of times a week. He seemed to be his usual self, as in not confiding in us as to what was going on. But, having said that that he must have been hurting deeply inside as Tony was his best friend! Perhaps if he had opened his heart out to us, I would have been more affected, but that's not how he or we, as a family, operated. When Joannie was there, we'd roll a joint or two and try and put the world to right. I wish I could tell you what our plans were to do that, but I was too stoned to remember…

Before, after and even during all this drama and uncertainty, there was one constant in our lives… and that was the traditional and elaborate Yuletide festivities at Eardley Crescent. One of Mum's gay friends, Martin Christopherson, was the 'window dresser' at Simpsons in Piccadilly, so he had a great sense of artistic flair. He was happy to decorate the quite large living/dining room into a beautiful warm Christmas theme and the plans for his designs were initiated a good couple of months before the day. It really was something to behold, almost like a set for a movie.

I was given the job of testing all the lights that were to go on the tree. In those days the bulbs were quite large and easily unscrewed to make sure they worked before being carefully arranged on the tree. Days before the Christmas event, Mum would go out and buy however many Christmas crackers she would need for the guests (normally in the region of twenty-four or so), unwrap them and add personalised little trinkets or gifts for each guest.

At that time the lodgers had mainly departed and we occupied most the house. Mum thus made use of the kitchen on the same floor as the living room and another tiny kitchen on the ground floor. Often she would start all the preparations days before using both kitchens. How she managed to feed all those people with everything that was associated with Christmas dinner was beyond me but that was just her. Her timing was ever perfect, as was her comedic nature. Apart from immediate family (which wasn't that many), she would invite some of the cast of the *Carry On* films.

Despite the presence of family and other friends, I suppose it would be fair to describe the event as a sort of 'Carry On Christmas' as lots of the company were guests every year. Altogether Mum appeared in seventeen *Carry On* films (four of them as the famed hospital matron) including the first, *Carry On Sergeant*, in 1958. Some years later, I passed my driving test and got my driving licence as a soon as humanly possible. Whenever I could, I used to chauffeur Mum anywhere she needed to go, as she didn't drive. As Mum was very much involved with The Leukemia Research Foundation, I used to take her to their charity shops where she worked behind the counter when she wasn't filming or doing the *Sykes* shows. Sometimes I would drive her to exterior locations where she would be ensconced for a couple of days and stay there and watch the process of making movies. It's very much like the music business, where the norm is, 'Hurry up and wait.' In the film biz there are long periods of time for set changes, costume changes perhaps, lights have to be repositioned as do the cameras. The actual shooting of the scene could last anything between thirty seconds to three minutes or more. Then you have to perform, be 'on' as it were. When we're on tour, sometimes there will be an early sound check because the doors might have to open earlier than usual for security reasons – particularly during these days of terrorist threats. So we might sound check at four in the afternoon but not go on stage 'till nine pm. So, hurry up and wait for nearly five hours!

Anyway, it was a pleasure to drive her around, and especially as we got on so well and enjoyed each other's company. I would take her to Pinewood Studios which is where all the *Carry On* films were made. In doing that I got to know all the cast members quite well, and it was a joy to see them and catch up. I had a bit of a crush on Shirley Eaton, but the beautiful Fenella Fielding, with that super sexy voice really knocked me over.

In talking to Jim Dale, we discovered a mutual interest in extraterrestrial life. He suggested I read *Chariots of the Gods*, which was written in 1968 by German author Erich von Däniken and poses the theory that the religions of ancient civilisations were formed by the visits of 'ancient astronauts', who were welcomed as gods. We talked about the possibility of other life in the universe at length. 'Extraterrestrial Life' is something I ponder a lot about. Not so much thin grey beings with large eyes but if there is any life out there. Some astronomers believe there are four hundred billion stars in our galaxy alone, and one hundred and seventy billion galaxies in the observable universe. Some of which have one hundred trillion stars. So, I think it's arrogant of us to believe we are the only life form in the universe. Who knows what kinds of life forms exist on planets that are in 'The Goldilocks Region' – where it's not too hot and not too cold, just the right distance from its sun.

I've actually seen a 'UFO'. I was on my way up to Bernie Taupin's ranch in California and I was sitting in the back seat of the car just gazing up at the blue sky when I saw a silver spherical object high up in the air. Now it wasn't moving, and it wasn't a weather balloon either. It was completely still. I couldn't take my eyes off it, then suddenly after about ten minutes or so it just vanished! I have no idea what it was, so I guess it was unidentifiable, at least to me. So that's my take on the question, and I'm open to any possibilities. And, no, I hadn't been on the vodka martinis.

Anyway, I really do digress – back to more earthly matters, although I'm still talking 'stars'; the *Carry On* cast were wonderful and always great fun at Christmas. Barbara Windsor, the lovely Sid James and I adored Kenneth Williams, who was a genius. Also, not many people know this, but he had an extensive knowledge of English history and he kept me enthralled. He actually never stopped talking and was always 'on', but was always erudite, witty and entertaining. He was a regular visitor to Eardley Crescent and he and Mum were as close as brother and sister yet he still kept a very private existence. I remember Mum only visited his flat once in all the time they knew each other. They were in a car together, close to his place and she needed to pee desperately.

Charlie, Kenny, Mum, Sid, Joan, Jim and Babs 'Carrying On'.

She pleaded with him to use his bathroom, but he was very unhappy to let her in – before finally agreeing to her increasingly frantic plight. He let her in to his flat, telling her she was one of the only people he had ever crossed the front door of his abode. She told me later that he lived an almost 'Spartan' existence – there was hardly any furniture although it was spotlessly clean. Most people thought that he was gay, but in fact he was really 'asexual'. I had never known him to have a partner, ever. In fact, he led a very lonely lifestyle.

Joan Sims was lovely but when she came to the house always had to bring her mother, Gladys, who was extremely overbearing and totally controlling over Joan. She made poor Joan's life hell and really wasn't a pleasant soul to be around. Every time Joan had a drink I could see her mother's disgust and sometimes Joan even had to hide her boyfriends and lovers from Gladys. Thinking back, I believe her mother was the cause of Joan's problem with alcohol. 'Nuff said about that…

On Christmas day itself, Bruce Copp would arrive at about 7am, always laden with half a dozen oysters and a half a bottle of champagne which he and Mum would term' breakfast'. Then the two of them would set to with the cooking. There were three kitchens in the house, each containing an oven and so three large turkeys could be roasted simultaneously.

The actual celebrations began about midday when guests started to arrive for the plentiful drinks and snacks. Mum and Martin always constructed an 'L' shaped table which looked amazing and so inviting with all the colourful candles, crackers bursting at the seams and gleaming glasses. The plates and silverware were all different sizes as she didn't have a matching service for everyone. The table groaned with all the food she had prepared, which was delicious. It was all perfect. The meal seemed to last for hours and everyone was in good spirits… except for Gladys.

After the meal, we usually played charades, which was loads of fun as there were so many people in 'the business' who were naturally great at all the miming and histrionics. The party often went late into the night with other guests dropping by after they had had their own celebrations. Boxing Day was like an extension of the day before – not quite as crazy, but still with lots of food and drinks. Mum always insisted that the decorations shouldn't be taken down until the Twelfth Night,

(5th January.) I've always thought this was quite a nice tradition. Here in America, Christmas is forgotten from 26th December. Over. Period! If you go to the supermarket even a couple of days after Christmas, you're bound to see displays for Valentine's Day. I'm sure it's a 'Hallmark' conspiracy.

In case you'd forgotten... and I wish I could... I was still at school. Although I didn't care for many of the staff, there was one teacher I got on with. He taught English. He was quite young and kind of 'hip' then. But when he knew that I had had enough of nine to four every day and told him I was going to leave in the summer of '69 and pursue music. He was appalled and told me I was making a big mistake... he was 'disappointed' in me. That actually hurt a little as I thought we got on quite well, but I suppose he was thinking of my best interests.

It's so true that whether your experience is happy or unhappy, schooldays have a profound effect on all of us. In my case I suffered from graphic, horrible nightmares for years and years. In my dreams I would be back at Westminster City School where I was being humiliated in various ways and I was stuck there with no escape. I felt as if I was in a prison. It was as if I had no future and would never be able to leave – like being in an eternal educational purgatory... going through the same routine over and over again and again.

One night after I had moved to Los Angeles in the 1970s, I had a dream about the school. I dreamt I had been invited back there and was given a tour of the school, its classrooms and an introduction to the teachers. It was almost as if I was some sort of celebrity being welcomed back and was asked to talk to the pupils and staff about my career. It was the only positive dream I ever had of the school and somehow I managed to impart some success from my subconscious into that dream. And since then, I've never had another nightmare about having to go back to school.

Around about this time, I also had a job at another famous institution, a club called The Scotch of St. James, off Piccadilly in London. The club opened in 1965 and was hidden away at the end of Mason's Yard, an unlikely alleyway to be a favoured hang out for rock stars. It was here that Jimi Hendrix first performed when he arrived in England the following year. The people who used to meet there are like a Who's Who of music legends and included Paul McCartney, The

Moody Blues, the Spencer Davis group, The Who and Stevie Wonder. The Beatles and the Stones were provided with their own private tables.

I was the resident DJ there for some months and the hours were very long there, but I earned good money. I used to get there about seven in the evening, have dinner which was part of my wage and then we opened at about eight o'clock. Part of my job description was to help the bands that were playing there by helping to bring their equipment in and out of the club.

The place was underground and sometimes a Hammond B3 organ, which was extremely heavy, had to be maneuvered down a spiral stairway. God knows I couldn't do that now, but in those days it didn't bother me. The best part of that job was choosing my own playlists. Surprisingly, I never had any complaints so I got away with listening to music that I loved for hours on end and way into the night. It's weird, I can't even remember how I got that gig. Of course by the time we were closing there was no public transport except for a couple of night buses that went nowhere close to home. So, I used so to share a taxi with a German girl who worked there as a waitress, an Amazonian type called Rita, who was about 6'4" in height. She lived not far from Eardley Crescent so it was quite convenient. I fancied her terribly but nothing ever came of that obsession. Probably too tall for me.

The summer of '69 was quite revealing, intoxicating, adventurous and more. I was sixteen then and the world was my clam, mussel and oyster. Exams, my GCSEs, weren't exactly uppermost in my mind. In fact they weren't in my mind at all. I left school while I was in the fifth form and so didn't have to take any. Mum had said I could leave when I wanted to and so I got out of the place as soon as I could.

I'd already been smoking hash/pot/cannabis, whatever you would like to call it – in those days it was risky, but it's funny that nowadays, if you get caught with a joint in the UK you just get a slap on the wrist. In the sixties, you were given a fine and perhaps a suspended sentence. Possession of more than an ounce and you ended up in prison.

The year of 1969 was also a landmark as it was then that I was introduced to LSD or acid as it was called at that time. The psychologist and writer Timothy Leary had first coined the phrase 'Turn on, tune in, drop out' at a hippy gathering in San Francisco's Golden Gate Park a couple of years before and now I was following his mantra. Well, I turned on and tuned in, but never really dropped out. The first time I took LSD, it really was a mind altering experience. The pill I took was called 'California Sunshine'. It was quite an amazing 'trip'. It made me feel so comfortable and complete. Lights and sounds were much more vivid and vibrant and I felt I could do anything. I loved it and this was actually the first of many 'trips'. I never had any side effects such as nausea or panic attacks and luckily I never had any 'bad trips' or negative experiences. The drug used to come in many forms in those days; pills, sugar cubes and small gelatin squares. They all had the same effect basically. Although I enjoyed taking LSD, I didn't indulge for too long and I stopped dropping acid as it lost its allure and novelty after a while. And I discovered that alcohol was more my hammer.

Not long after knowing that I would never have to step over the portals of Westminster Grammar again, I had the confidence to apply for a place at The Royal College of Music of all places. I got an audition and despite my lack of academic achievements, they seemed to like the way I could play the guitar. I was actually offered a place at the celebrated 'conservatoire'. (Yes, that's how they describe themselves).

Mum actually tried to discourage me from having anything to do with the music business or its peripheries. She was worried about the insecurities of the job, although, of course, she and Dad were in the most insecure of professions. This attempt at guiding me on the right career path – or at least avoiding the wrong one – lasted about five minutes when Mum realised this is what I wanted to do. 'Are you sure this is what you want to do?'

She went on to explain that her agent, Felix de Wolfe, had a brother who ran a music licensing company (De Wolfe Music) and she could ask about getting a job with them. I told her that I appreciated her helping me, but it just wasn't for me. That was the end of the discussion and thankfully both she and Dad were totally supportive when they realised I had set my heart on being a musician. My dad was very musical. In fact I always believed he'd have preferred to have earned a living playing the piano rather than acting. But in later years, they both became immensely proud that I was doing what I loved to do and was able to earn a living from it.

I knew the composer and musician Mike Batt, who lived around the corner and, through him, hung out with other musicians, a couple with whom he had been to school. That summer I met two brothers, Tim (guitar) and Andy Renton (drums), who were to become firm friends. They had played in their first gigs as teenagers in local community halls and schools in and around Winchester, where they grew up. While studying at Art College in Brighton, Tim had formed a band, Ka, with some mates. Their manager advised that they would have to go to London to play better venues and get noticed. Tim duly gave up his course, but some of the band were unable to move to the capital and so they needed to recruit a singer and a bass player.

Andi Banks, who was both a vocalist and a bass player, was a friend of mine and had been recommended to Tim. I had met Andi through John Schofield, who managed Spirit of Essence, the band that Andi was in. John had suggested to Andi that I help record the band one evening at The Pheasantry, a famous club in the King's Road. I had organised the sound equipment and then when Andi found out that I played guitar, suggested I sit in with him on the gig. We became great mates straightaway, but he knew very little about me, when early on in our friendship, he crashed at Eardley Crescent after a particularly heavy night of getting stoned.

The following morning I had to wake him early because I had to go to school! I'll never forget the look on his face when he saw me in school uniform. Andi, who was several years older than me, assumed we were the same age and was astonished that I was still in full time education. He thought that I rented a flat in the house. I told him not to rush, to help himself to some food from the kitchen and to make himself at home. Andi did just this and explored upstairs. He found an air rifle (I can't recall who owned that) and seeing a traffic warden in the street below, 'fired' the unloaded rifle at the warden from the window overlooking Eardley Crescent. The warden was disturbed by the sound of the rifle going off, but each time Andi ducked under the window unseen.

Andi was just cocking the gun again when he heard a voice behind him, 'What on earth do you think you're doing?' Andi was a fan of the *Carry On* films and recognised the voice immediately. It was my mum, of course. Not only was he shocked to be discovered behaving badly in someone else's house, but it just happened to be by Hattie Jacques of all people. He had no idea she was my mother. He sheepishly apologised and admitted, 'I'm pretending to shoot the traffic warden.' 'Oh, jolly good,' Mum replied and left the room without any further questions as to why, who he was or what he was doing in the house. According to Andi it was never mentioned again. Andi ended up living with us for a while and actually drove my mum around for a while when he discovered that her Daimler was mainly unused and he had a driving licence.

Anyway, Andi brought me along to meet the Rentons at the Bunch of Grapes pub on the Knightsbridge's Brompton Road. Tim recalls Andi saying to him, 'Well, I'll join if Robin joins.' And we did. We became 'Reign'. Tim, who was also older than me, had been hugely influenced by the Shadows and the very early bluesmen of the late 50s early 60s such as Cyril Davies Band and Steampacket. I came from a later generation of Eric Clapton, Jimmy Page and Jimi Hendrix and so we had completely different styles. With my penchant for the blues – even at the age of sixteen – we created music that was quite eclectic.

Reign at the Greyhound, London. Andy Renton, Debi Doss, Dave Thomas, myself and a surprised Tim Renton (TIM RENTON)

A fan of Reign, Peter Johnson, put some money into the band and purchased a huge PA system, which he hired out with other equipment when we weren't working. Brother Jake and another friend called Chris Warwick acted as roadies for various bands, including The Drifters. We did get some gigs around London and hoping to get gigs further afield, our publicist, Flavia Irons, suggested we go to the South of France scouting for gigs. We drove there in a Mini, listening all the way to the Stones on an 8 track cartridge. We stayed with my uncle Robin at his place in the medieval hillside village of Bormes-les-Mimosa in Provence. A beautiful spot. It was a great trip, but I don't think we actually managed to procure any work. It was only when I got back that I discovered that she had ulterior motives for the expedition, but actually nothing happened. Can't remember why not.

We did, however, gig at a USAF base in Germany and I had a transit van with airline seats. The van's rear differential had gone and we had to endure a terrible screaming noise all the way to Frankfurt. We were stopped and searched regularly by the police – perhaps it was the noise from the differential that attracted them.

Reign had somehow got involved with Mike Smith, who was the saxophone player with the group Amen Corner. Mike now called himself 'a producer' and he actually managed to get us a recording deal with Regal Zonophone, one of EMI's labels at the time. I now had to make the choice of whether to take up my place at The Royal College of Music or stick with Reign and sign a recording deal. It wasn't that difficult a decision. In fact it was a 'no brainer'. It was rock 'n' roll. And, so, at the tender age of sixteen, I had turned professional.

Just before the recording deal came up, I went across the Atlantic for the first time. Mum occasionally did a show in Toronto, a variety series for Canadian television. Hosted by John Hewer, a stalwart and friend of Mum's from the Players', it was called *The Pig and Whistle* and set in a fictionalised English pub.

When I returned to England early in 1970, it was time to get to work on our first record. Mike Smith wanted us to record a song, 'Line of Least Resistance', written by Keith Relf and Jim McCarty of The Yardbirds fame. 'Not a bad start,' I thought. Plus, we were to record at the legendary Abbey Road Studios – in the same studio as The Beatles. I borrowed a 12 string which belonged to the guitarist from Chicken

Shack and we used Ringo's Gretch drum kit to boot! Looking back, this was quite an amazing start for a teenager, not long out of school. (The 'B' side was titled, 'Natural Lovin' Man'). I remember we had just finished the recording when Andi came into the studio and announced that the London Evening Papers had just reported the news that Jimi Hendrix had been found dead. We were all shattered, as all of us were huge Hendrix fans.

I was very proud of our single and it still sounds good to me. Unfortunately it got lost in the quagmire of others being released at the same time. The record barely received any air play and we didn't have any promotion. And, the icing on the cake was Mike Smith lost all interest and seemed to disappear off the planet. Recording deal? Ha! This promise was one of the scams that used to happen to so many young groups in the sixties. 'The producer' would sign to the label and give a pittance to the group after they had signed to him, but would never really deliver. But, I didn't care at the time. They were still great days. I met the wonderfully named Zally Caws when she was going out with Andi. Zally became a very close friend and she used to hang out a lot at Eardley Crescent through the years. We are still in touch and Zally has just retired from running her own graphic design business.

We played as much as we could and anywhere we could. We didn't have management or an agent so it was up to us to find the gigs, which we did somehow, performing at least twice a week for several years. These were mostly at small clubs up and down the country but we also appeared at various universities. We supported Genesis at Surrey University, the Kinks at Kent and at a couple of Oxford University May Balls where we opened for Family and the Moody Blues. We also played a few times at legendary Soho venues such as *the Marquee* and *Ronnie Scott's*.

There were so many clubs in those days, but now sadly so many of them have gone. Even the famous Marquee Club on Wardour St in London's Soho district closed in 1988. There's nothing really left of the place now except for a 'Blue Plaque' which states 'Keith Moon played here'. A nice tribute but it was such an important venue I'm surprised there is nothing else. I loved playing there! I used to go to go there so often to see so many groups there, mostly the guys who were playing blues and rhythm and blues and bands like Fleetwood Mac and Ten

Years After. It was run by John Gee and Jack Barry, a couple of queens and I'm sure they fancied me as I don't remember ever paying to get through the front door. Great nights were spent there.

If I remember correctly, Jack also had a club called La Chasse just up the street, above The Ship pub in Soho's Wardour Street, where I used to go to after the shows at the club were over. And then there was The Speakeasy on Margaret St. It was a late night club and restaurant and like The Scotch was frequented by all the greats in those days such as David Bowie, Pink Floyd, Jeff Beck and inevitably Jimi Hendrix and The Who.

We played a there a few times. I remember a tiny stage, but 'The Speak' as most people called it in the day was very prestigious. The guy at the door was an Italian called Mino who always greeted me with much enthusiasm – I never really knew why, but I gratefully accepted his hospitality. The restaurant was very good, run by another Italian, Luigi. He was a miserable sod – never smiled and always wore a grumpy face which, for some reason, people seemed to like. He was, thankfully, a fantastic chef, who put his emotional energy and skill into making the most incredible food. He made the best beef stroganoff I've ever had even though, when he served the Hungarian dish, he almost threw it on the table. I played there a few times over the years. Once, at the bar I recognised Ritchie Blackmore – the songwriter and guitarist from Deep Purple and I told him, 'You're one of my favourite guitar players.' Ritchie wasn't impressed and gave me a cold stare. I suppose I should have said he was my most favourite guitarist. I slunk away. Some years later I was in a hotel bar with Zally Caws when this guy approached, greeted me very warmly, 'Hi Robin, how are you doing? What are you up to?' I had no idea who he was and turned to Zally for help. She looked very impressed, but I said to him, 'I'm sorry, do I know you?' He smiled and replied, 'I'm Rick, Rick Parfitt.' And it was the famous 'Quo' songwriter and guitarist. I was very embarrassed, but Rick was quite unconcerned and absolutely charming. Very different from Ritchie Blackmore. A sad loss.

Andi Banks, who remains a close mate, left Reign due to other commitments and we worked with a number of different male and female vocalists. Here are some memories from Shirley Roden: 'I met Robin Le Mesurier in the early 1970s when I joined the group Reign as a singer alongside Dave Thomas and Debi Doss. Robin was a great guitarist to have in the band as he was always innovative, stylish and a wonderfully creative musician with tons of talent, dedication and real passion and vision for the music we were creating, as well as a good sense of humour (invaluable when you are working so closely together!). I always remember him with sparkly shirts and his flying V guitar (with the beautiful beaded guitar-strap Debi made for him); sweat dripping of his back hair as he blasted out those high-speed guitar solos! I loved working with Robin as he always lifted the music with the intensity of every chord he played and he added so much visually to the stage too. Reign was an interesting band to be in. We may not have ultimately made the big time, but we certainly did some great gigs and I loved the time I spent in the band and with Robin.'

The band spent a lot of time at Eardley Crescent – in fact it was an open house and some used to stay with us regularly. Andy Renton lived with us for a while as did Chris Warwick, our sound engineer. Mum would be on hand to provide meals at all times of the day and night. She was very liberal and she would put up with much more miscreant behaviour than any other parent I knew. She also gave some of them work employing them as 'chauffeurs' driving her to work and charity events as well as gainfully employing them in Grandma Mary's house in Waterford Road, Fulham. Tim Renton once drove Mary to a production of *Charley's Aunt* at BBC Television Centre at White City in which Mum was appearing. The officious commissioners wouldn't let Tim into the car park and when Mary said she was Hattie Jacques's mother, they were very rude and didn't believe her. Mum was furious when she found out later what had happened. The BBC commissioners were infamous at that time for being obstructive – particularly at Television Centre which they guarded with fearsome officiousness.

Being in the band was a great experience and I had a lot of fun cutting my teeth in the rock and roll world. It was a wonderful time, but only for a short time. Unfortunately our particular Reign ended after only three years – we didn't last nearly as long as HM Queen Elizabeth II.

4

UNWOMBLISH BEHAVIOUR

On the Christmas of 1973, Mike Batt asked Tim and Andy Renton if members of Reign could come and 'fill some costumes' of a group of furry creatures known as The Wombles. The Wombles looked like oversized rodents, but not ugly – sort of cuddly and cute – and were inspired by Elisabeth Beresford's children's books. The engagement was for a song during the interval of The Eurovision Song Contest that was due to take place in Brighton the following spring.

Eurovision 1974 turned out to be quite a momentous occasion as it was the year that ABBA were victorious with 'Waterloo'. I seem to recall they did quite well after that. We had great fun being filmed collecting rubbish in the grounds of the Brighton pavilion, careering around the pier in a speedboat and driving around neighbouring cliff tops in dune buggies – there aren't actually many sand dunes in Brighton.

This event was actually the first television appearance of the Wombles but Mike had initially become involved when he had been asked to write a theme song for the children's BBC television programme, which was then a five minute show and about some imaginary creatures that lived underneath Wimbledon Common and whose occupation was to clean up all the litter that humans had left behind. 'The Wombling Song' was a huge hit in England and Mike had the idea of putting a group together to promote the record. So he got his occasional seamstress mum to make the furry costumes for us all to wear on the many TV shows on which we duly appeared.

The Wombles were a huge success thanks to the many hits that Mike wrote. At one stage the group had two albums and two singles in the charts – even though we didn't play on these. We did so many shows such as *Blue Peter*, *Crackerjack*, and about ten appearances on *Top Of the Pops*. Most of these were pre-recorded, although we did play live on occasions. There was one *TOTP* in which Stevie Wonder appeared. He actually played a few songs live in rehearsal and during the recording, but virtually no-one was listening to him play. Incredible! It was in those days I became friends with the guys from the likes of The Bay City Rollers, Mud, Sweet and Slade.

We even went abroad and worked on a television show with the James Last orchestra. ABBA happened to be on the same show and we knew them a little as, apart from Eurovision, we'd done so many *Top Of The Pops* with them in the past. I have to say they were so charming and I developed an immediate crush on Agnetha Fältskog. The television show was typically German, a kind of variety show with quite a few home grown artists, none of which I'd ever heard of. There was much lederhosen and a lot of slapping of thighs. At that time I made friends with one of the record company executives called Renata Damm. She invited me to stay over with her in Frankfurt for a few days and as there was nothing workwise on the horizon for the next week or so I was more than happy to spend time with her. She was a lovely girl; very pretty, pale skinned and with bright red hair. Anyone would take one look at her and swear she was Irish. It was nothing more than a friendship and sadly I never saw her again after that trip.

It's difficult to believe but Womble mania really did exist. Mike Batt was quoted as saying, 'It was like being Clark Kent and Superman. Nobody cared if they saw me wander down the street, but if I was dressed as Orinoco, they were all over me.' The merchandising was hugely successful. We opened a record shop in Ealing Broadway which Peter Sellers attended. Tim recalls how the women were drawn to him. Mind you he didn't have much competition from us Wombles. One July, we were even asked to open a supermarket in Manchester and about 10,000 people turned up. We weren't even performing! We just stood there, hardly being able to see anything through the tiny peep holes inside the uncomfortably hot and very heavy fake fur costumes. We were boiling to death in the heat, while signing autographs and having our pictures taken. But it was a living at the time, and not a bad one to be honest.

Because of our popularity, there was great speculation about the identities of the musicians. For those in the know we could be recognised by our instruments; Andy Renton obviously on drums, Tim playing his Rickenbacker and me with my Flying V, but for those outside the organisation, this conjecture went on for quite some time.

At one point some savvy journalist from one of the tabloids discovered that I was a Womble. I was 'Wellington' to be precise. And, for what it's worth, I'd like to point out that the bespectacled Wellington was considered to be the brightest of all the Wombles! Anyway, Mum and I were coerced into doing a photo shoot and an interview. Our secret was out and although we weren't supposed to talk to the press, we got away with it that time.

I was a Womble for a couple of years until one night when I was returning home from a television recording and spotted a policeman's helmet through a window on the first floor. 'Hello, hello, hello,' I thought... 'what's all this then?' It turned out that 67 Eardley Crescent was being raided!

I went in and discovered that there were four policemen, two policewomen and a dog in the house.

One of the officers accosted me, 'We heard your brother is a dealer.'

'No way,' I replied. 'He's not a dealer.'

'Well, we have it on good authority.'

'That's ridiculous!'

They turned the place upside down and inside out looking for drugs. Carpets were torn back, every single drawer and cupboard was searched and even some of the garden was dug up. Mum was even strip searched, which was incredibly humiliating for her. The police were there for hours and all they found was one 'joint' that belonged to Jake. I could tell at the time they were really pissed off not having found anything else. Later on, Mike Batt light-heartedly reported that the joint was hidden in one of the Wombles' heads and although this was funny, it wasn't true!

A mutual friend of mine and Jake's was at the house at the time, and eventually the three of us were taken to the local police station and charged with possession of a Class B illegal drug. While we were there, I asked... no... pleaded with the sergeant in charge to make sure that the incident wasn't leaked to the press. I wanted to protect Mum as she was very well known by then and this sort of publicity could be damaging. But of course within a day the story was all over the newspapers under the banner headline, 'Unwomblish Behaviour'. Never trust a copper in a situation like that. I wonder how much someone was paid to leak the story.

A few weeks later we had to go to court to answer the charge. In the meantime, a solicitor was procured for the three of us. We met and 'The Brief' told us just to plead guilty as were likely only to receive a small fine. So we did and the fine, if I remember correctly, was £10 each. In retrospect I should have pleaded not guilty as the substance wasn't mine. In fact I had nothing to do with it. I suppose when I saw the police in the house, I should have just taken off and come back later, but I didn't. I suppose I'd got a bit of a shock by their presence in our house and somehow wanted to help.

But the fine was the least if it. Because of pleading guilty to possession of drugs, I now had a criminal record. In later years, the arrest made it difficult for me to get working visas for the US and affected my application for a green card (as a permanent resident) when I later wanted to live in the USA.

And there was an even more immediate punishment. A couple of days after the article appeared in the newspaper, I got an apologetic call from Mike Batt, telling me that the Wombles' creator, Elisabeth Beresford, had decided I shouldn't be associated with the children's books and so I was not suitable to be a part of the group. I was stunned that this incident, in which I was totally innocent, could have such an outcome. I had lost a very lucrative job, but that was that. I was no longer a Womble...

Funnily enough The Wombles reformed and actually played Glastonbury in 2011 – more than I've ever done. When I was with the group, there was one very strange experience that seemed inexplicable at the time. We had appeared on the magazine programme *Pebble Mill at One* and got up early to set up. I drove the Renton brothers to the studio in Birmingham, but on the way back, I fell asleep at the wheel. It could only have been for a moment, but I heard a voice screaming at me, 'Robin! Robin!'

I woke up immediately with a jolt and screeched to a halt. I turned around to thank the guys for waking me up and saving my life, but they were all fast asleep and completely oblivious of the danger that we had been in. I couldn't work it out. I had definitely heard my name being yelled. I drove home very carefully for the rest of the journey, but was so traumatised by what had happened that there was no chance of me dropping off again. Later I thought about that voice and suddenly realised that this was a female voice... and it belonged to my Uncle Robin's first wife, Azetta Jacques (nee Van Der Merwe), a South African model for *Vogue* and William Hartnell. She had died in 1958 – long before this incident.

Some years later, a friend called Patricia, who claimed to be a psychic, once pointed to a photograph of Azetta and stated, 'She's your Guardian Angel!' Patricia had no idea about the near fatal car crash and then I began to think more about her. When Mum was living in Eardley Crescent sometimes when alone she would hear a voice calling, 'Jo! Jo!' which, as I explained earlier, was Hattie's real name and only her family and closest friends knew. Could this have been Azetta? My bedroom at Eardley Crescent was directly above Mum's and there was one occasion when mum heard footsteps above her in the middle of the night and came to check what I was doing and enquire as to why I was up at that time. I was in bed, awake and also heard the footsteps, but wasn't at all scared. I'm sure now it was Azetta keeping an eye on me and that she has helped me throughout my life. I always seemed to be in the right place at the right time. Part of my 'charmed life'.

Tim Renton was also sacked from The Wombles – there was an agreement that we shouldn't talk to the press and that our real identities should be kept secret, but he became fed up with this lack of recognition and that other people, non musicians, were being employed. (Mike Batt had the rights to the characters and so the band had no control over what happened). Tim spoke to the *Daily Express*, spilt the beans and inevitably also received the 'Thank you and goodbye' call from Mike. Tim's only regret was that his sacking happened just before a tour of the USA! For those of you who don't know... Tim was Uncle Bulgaria (And Tim's wife, Sandy, was Madame Cholet on occasions).

Azetta, my 'Guardian Angel' (JOHN PAUL JACQUES)

In 1975, Tim, brother, Andy and I and a very talented singer/ songwriter named Brian Engel put a new group together called Shambles. Incidentally, 'Shambles' is the very old name for a slaughterhouse! If you ever visit 'The Shambles' in York, the name does not refer to the muddled nature of the buildings, it derives from the site of an old slaughterhouse that it's built on. History lesson over.

Brian wrote songs in the style of Lol Crème of 10cc and had just appeared in the film version of *The Rocky Horror Picture Show*. We recorded one single, produced by Roy Thomas Baker (of Queen fame) titled 'Hello Baby' for CBS. It was a good pop song but never really got anywhere. Tim and Andy left the band. For the record, Tim, an architect by trade, formed an excellent band called 3am about ten years ago and they play regularly in England.

Shambles morphed into Limey, which was mainly formed from the survivors of a short lived group called Stryder. The line-up at the time was Brian, vocals, Ian Kewley, keyboards, Dave Bowker, bass, Ian McInerney, drums and me. We signed to RCA Records which was when I made my first ever album, *Jack Union*. We recorded it at the newly completed Roundhouse Studios, in north London. It was, I believe, the first studio in London that had in-house catering. We were soon to go on the road to promote the album and opened up for Andy Fairweather Low, who at the time had a huge hit with 'Wide Eyed and Legless'. Andy was originally in Amen Corner and I've never been sure if they took the name from the novel by Rick Shefchik or the area in south London. In later years he played with Eric Clapton for some considerable time. Anyhow, before the tour started we were ensconced for two weeks rehearsing in a cricket pavilion and staying at a bed and breakfast establishment near Reading – about forty miles from London.

The B&B was run by quite an elderly couple. The wife was very sweet and friendly, but her husband was a grumpy old bugger. Every morning we would have breakfast together. There was the usual fare of cereal, tea and toast, plus a hot breakfast (not the 'full' English) of scrambled eggs and bacon. There was a little serving hatch that separated the breakfast room from the kitchen through which, every morning, the old man would poke his head and pose the question, 'Beans or tomatoes?' He was quite threatening in a way. Anyway, we would either ask for one or the other. On the last day we were there, the usual question was asked, to which I summoned up the courage to reply, 'I'd like both please.' 'Both?' He repeated aggressively. 'Yes, both, please, I responded somewhat falteringly. I felt like Oliver Twist asking, 'Please sir, could I have some more?' The landlord looked a bit taken aback, but surprisingly agreed. So I got both beans and tomatoes to my delight and to the shock of the others.

Our road crew then consisted of Malcolm Culmore, Patrick Logue, who was nicknamed 'Boiler' and Tommy Willis who was also a rather good guitarist too. Tommy once told me he was hung by his ankles out of a window for some time by one of the Kray brothers (the most feared and respected gang leaders in London during the 60s) for something very innocuous. He told me that he was sure that was going to be the end of him, but he somehow survived.

Mal and Boiler were to become very dear and important to me in the future. Malcolm had scoliosis so badly, and in fact as a child, the doctors said he might not make it past his tenth birthday but he was always very determined to prove the medics wrong. He was an incredibly dogged character, a truly hard worker and always very loyal.

It was at this time that I became involved with Myra Chronin, my first proper girlfriend. Well… technically she was Brian Engel's girlfriend and actually his cohabitee, but they seemed to have an open relationship and both of them were having affairs. Myra and I were friends initially, but then romance blossomed. She used to work at Biba, London's trendiest fashion store, as a graphic artist and we would meet most lunch times for amorous trysts when Brian was otherwise occupied.

A group of us; Andi Banks, Zally Caws, Brian and Myra once rented a cottage in the Lake District, near Ullswater. It was soon after I had embarked on my fling with Myra and at that time Brian didn't know anything about us carrying on. One afternoon, I made it clear to the others, who were aware of our affair, that I would like to be left alone with Myra. So they dutifully all went for a walk on the fells and persuaded Brian to accompany them. Brian was wearing his platform boots, which were then fashionable but totally unsuitable for the terrain. They set off, while Myra and I began to take advantage of a little privacy but unknown to us, they hadn't got very far (and neither had Myra and I) when Brian broke one of his heels. He couldn't continue on the walk and so the group headed for home… and us.

Zally made sure that Brian went as slowly as possible, distracting him with discourses on nature, scenery, the history of the Lakes and anything she could to delay his arrival back at the cottage. Meanwhile Andi raced around on another path in order to warn us. By the time the group arrived back at the cottage, Myra and I were sitting down to a very sedate game of scrabble. Thanks folks!

There was another trip to the Lakes when we visited Mum who was in summer season with Eric Sykes at Blackpool, renting Sir Stanley Matthews' house and she arranged for us all to go riding. Zally had never been on a horse before and was a little nervous about the whole outing. I was quite confident and explained to Zally that the way to get the horse's trust is to hold a sugar lump in your open palm and the horse will take it gently from your hand. So, I put a sugar lump in my hand and the horse nuzzled my hand for the sugar lump and then took a great bite out of my hand, leaving me bruised and bleeding. I wasn't best pleased and I don't think it did much for Zally's confidence.

While we were in Blackpool, we visited a palm reader, who told me I'd be going on a long trip overseas – just before I ended up living in Los Angeles, which impressed me a bit. The Gypsy lady told Zally that she could picture her sitting in a chair on a luxurious red carpet, excitedly calling out, 'I've done it! I've done it!' Zally is apparently still waiting for that scene to come to fruition and hasn't, as far as she knows, 'done it!'

Sorry, I've lost my place… oh yes… Brian soon cottoned on to the fact that Myra and I were having a fling and in the end accepted it all with good grace. The affair went on for about a year but then Myra and Brian split up and she moved to the USA. Not only did I lose Myra, but the band also disbanded. We'd made a second album for RCA called *Silver Eagle*, but the group was already falling apart. Not a good time.

I was doing a lot of sessions in London in those days, a big chunk for Micky Most, already established as a very famous record producer and the head of Rack Records. I was very lucky as not many session players got to work with him. It was great fun and we spent hours chatting about this and that – mostly music and wine. Being a session guitarist was a great learning curve because of the myriad of artists I played with including Cat Stevens (now Yusuf Islam), Suzi Quatro, and Lulu. Sometimes, I would be called in to do a backing track and didn't even know who I was recording for!

I then joined Stryder – a reincarnation of the original band, who used to open for The Faces. We had a great time playing around the country with Mal and Boiler taking care of our gear and a guy called Jack Noton driving us. As you can probably imagine, in those days, there was much misconduct and mischief occurring on our travels. We had to be very careful about having any drugs on us. The police at that time used to love to bust anyone in the music business. So we were very cautious from past experiences. It was mostly girls, alcohol and… more girls.

It was usually Boiler or Mal who found us the groupies and invited them to our hotel. Sounds so old fashioned now but that was the way it was all those years ago. Seemed quite harmless then. And they were all of a certain age I'd like to add. We had fun, they had fun. We left the next day to move on to another town, and that was that. I'll say no more... only to protect the innocent. Not that I can remember any names of the 'innocents' although I'm sure there are still Polaroid prints floating about.

I met Pete Buckland at a Stryder gig at the Marquee in 1974. He was to become a very important figure in my life – both professionally and personally. He was originally an apprentice engineer, but was a real music fan and got to know musicians by attending gigs at various London clubs. He became a mate of Aynsley Dunbar's and became a roadie for Jeff Beck. Pete then worked with The Faces, doing a bit of everything – tour manager, sound mixer and front of house sound. For the last fifteen years he has managed Diana Krall's tours.

Following the demise of the Faces, Pete was now working with Rod Stewart and was putting a crew together for Rod's first solo worldwide tour, which was to commence in November 1976. Malcolm Culmore and Boiler were involved but Pete also needed a guitar tech as there were three guitarists in the band (Jim Cregan, Gary Grainger and Billy Peek). Pete asked me if I'd be interested. The job would mean that I would be setting up the amps and tuning the guitars. It wasn't really what I wanted to do but I didn't think I'd ever get the chance to travel throughout Europe before going to Australia, New Zealand and Hawaii. It was an opportunity not to be missed – so I agreed.

The band rehearsed at one of the sound stages of Shepperton film studios for a fortnight before travelling to Trondheim in Norway where the first gig was due to take place at the beginning of November. Unfortunately this was the start of winter and Trondheim is only about two hundred miles from the Arctic Circle. It was bitterly cold and the weather was so awful that nearly every vehicle broke down in the freezing conditions. The dates in Scandinavia were hard work, but the promise of warmer climes in January made it seem worthwhile. It was frustrating for me that I wasn't playing although I jammed with the band while we were doing sound checks and it was then that Rod heard me playing – something that was going to make a huge difference to my career later on. Jim Cregan also recently recalled that when I was tuning his guitar, I used to play his parts, note for note, and that I sometimes played them better than him. I'm not sure about that, but it was very kind of him to say so!

We continued to play further Scandinavian dates in Sweden and Denmark and one gig in Amsterdam before returning to England. We were booked in for four nights at Olympia in London towards the end of December and I remember at one of those concerts, Mum came to the show and sat next to Elton John. Elton was freaking out because he was sitting next to Hattie Jacques and Mum was freaking out that she happened to be sitting next to Elton John!

Rod wanted to celebrate Hogmanay in Scotland and so we all went to Glasgow and played two nights there. We were staying at the Albany hotel when the police raided our rooms on 4th January 1977. It was very weird why we should be raided (must have been the same informer who tipped the police off about Jake) and Rod wasn't even there. The police found a little marijuana and charged a number of us including the monitor engineer called Jim and Billy Peek, who never smoked and is as straight as the day is long. It transpired his enema bag was mistaken by the officers as some sort of drug paraphernalia. A mistake anyone could make if not properly trained! We spent the day in the cells and were then rushed to the Apollo Theatre under police escort for the show. The locals had become restless when the show was delayed and the police realised it was in their best interests to get us to the venue as safely and quickly as possible.

In an edition of *The Sun* two days later a banner headline ran 'MR MONEY PAYS AS ROD'S MEN ARE FINED' and the piece described how 'Top pop aide Peter Buckland sat in court with a box full of money yesterday'. The cash was actually stashed in a silver Halliburton suitcase.

The article continued, 'And as four members of singer Rod Stewart's entourage were fined a total of £225 on drugs charges he peeled off £5 and £10 notes and paid on the spot. Then Mr Buckland walked down a corridor to the bail office at Glasgow Sherriff Court and shelled out cash to bail seven others... among them was Robin Le Mesurier, the 23-year-old son of *Dad's Army* star John Le Mesurier. He was fined £75 after admitting possessing cannabis. The court was told that Le Mesurier is a road manager with the group and also a talented musician.' Mmmm...

We had actually had a bit of fun at the hotel with an aging and sozzled security guard, who had fallen asleep in the hallway and we gaffer taped him to his chair. Maybe that's what we should have been arrested for.

In February 1977 the band travelled to Australia and one of the first gigs was in Perth. To my delight I discovered that Dad was appearing there in a production of *The Miser*. It even transpired that we were staying at the same hotel. It was such a lovely coincidence. Dad used to sit in the bar in his bedroom slippers and call everyone 'darling', which everyone found charming. One evening after both shows, a couple approached him and asked if he was really John Le Mesurier and, if so, could they have his autograph? Gary Grainger, one of the band members, asked my dad how it felt to be famous and to be bothered by people all the time. Dad replied, 'Oh, I'm very happy to be asked politely for autographs. It's quite simple, you see, the two of them could have seen me and said, "Oh look there's John Le Mesurier... Fuck him!"'

When we arrived in Sydney, the temperature was 114 degrees. It was blistering! We had a few days off and stayed at the Sebel TownHouse Hotel in Sydney, which in the mid 1960s, had gained quite a reputation for its customer care and meeting any request – no matter how outlandish – from its guests. More importantly the staff turned a blind eye to any bad behaviour or excesses and so the Sebel became a favourite haunt of entertainers and musicians and claimed to be 'one of the world's great rock and roll hotels'. Sadly the hotel closed in 2000 and the building was developed into luxury apartments.

My closest pal on the tour was the lighting designer Patrick Woodroffe and during the day, we'd hang out by the pool on the roof. Patrick had read somewhere that the way of developing a perfect tan was to cover yourself with olive oil and iodine. And that's exactly what we did. We sprayed each other with this concoction. We must have been out of our minds! 'Mad Dogs and Englishmen' as the Noel Coward lyric goes.

In the evenings we'd hang out in the Round Bar where the walls were coved in photos of celebrities. There was much drinking and smoking of pot. I loved being there in the height of summer and there weren't that many shows so we had quite a lot of spare time. I was also lucky in that I had Mal and Boiler to bounce off and, at that time, Rod was with

Britt Ekland who I'd met years before when she was married to Peter Sellers. So Britt was yet another pal to hang out with on the road.

From there we moved on to New Zealand and then to Hawaii where we stayed at the Kahala Hilton. Hawaii was great and Patrick reminded me recently that all he can remember were the sunsets and the girls – although not necessarily in that order. I suppose it hit us that there we were, touring with such a successful artist, which was an exciting new experience for us both. We were young, handsome, without fear and having the times of our lives.

Patrick Woodroffe and I decided to travel around the USA for a while when the tour ended, starting in Los Angeles. I had never been to the 'City of Angels' before and was keen to experience a little bit of California, where so much good music had come from. As we were about to land in LA something extraordinary happened, which I just couldn't explain; I had this totally overwhelming feeling I was coming home. I'd never set foot there and yet I immediately felt a bond with the city. I just couldn't explain it. Nevertheless that's how I felt. Patrick and I stayed with two girls who worked for the aptly named 'Avalon Attractions', a company that promoted Rod and they showed us the sights – in all possible senses. My feeling for the city intensified and I knew that one day this would be my home.

Patrick and I rented a car and drove up the coast to Santa Barbara – a beautiful town nestling along the Pacific coast with a particularly Spanish feel – a historic mission and chock full of whitewashed buildings with vibrant red tiled roofs. I was introduced to someone who had a music shop there on State Street and discovered guitars galore in the store. I found an iconic guitar in the shape of a '62 Sunburst Fender Stratocaster for the unbelievably low price of $280. I bought it without a second thought but sadly it was stolen some years later. If one wanted to buy the same model these days it would be in the region of $40,000! But I played it for years with great pleasure. I miss that one. By the way, when I arrived back at Heathrow the customs agent didn't believe the price I paid and wanted to see 'the real receipt'. I told him this was the genuine receipt and after some time he begrudgingly let me through.

We travelled to St. Louis to see and stay with Debbie Villareal, a friend of Debi Doss, who hailed from St. Louis and was one of the 'back up' singers in Reign along with Shirley Roden. Debbie was very gregarious and had a great sense of humour. She and her friend Donna took us all around St. Louis, and introduced us to lots of interesting restaurants. We went to one place that was famous for their ribs. It was in a slightly seedy part of the city but the food was amazing. She also took us to a hamburger eatery called 'White Castle', a chain which was founded in Wichita in 1921. The restaurants were built to look like mini castles and they served tiny hamburgers, which in 1921 cost 5 cents but in the late 1970s we had to pay 50 cents apiece. We had to buy at least four of them to make a proper meal. They were the original 'sliders' which are now considered as gourmet finger food.

We took a ride up to the top of the famous Gateway Arch in St. Louis. Not something I would do again as I've since developed a fear of heights. We also took a few road trips and drove to Chicago, stopping briefly at Normal and Peoria on the way. I seem to remember visiting a museum then having a late lunch in Chicago at a place called 'Lettuce Entertain You'. Ha!

Patrick and I stayed in New York for a week with a friend of Mum's. A rather plump old queen called Alan Morton Walker. I can't recall how they met, or became friends but they were very close. Alan told us that he worked for the US government stocking US army bases, called PXs, all over the world. It sounded like a legitimate job, but Mum and I always thought he was in the CIA. Alan lived on 2nd and 47th Street, very close to the UN building, in a skyscraper apartment full of camp curios and dark Chinese furniture. It certainly wasn't particularly swish, especially when I caught a cockroach climbing up my right leg! My first ever encounter with an American 'roach'. I was horrified but was told, 'Don't worry, they don't bite.' But still… WTF?

I took great pleasure in exploring New York during that stay. Of course we did the usual touristy things; viewing The Statue of Liberty, ascending to the top of The Empire State Building and exploring Central Park among other sights, but almost every day, I spent hours playing different guitars through various amplifiers at Manny's, the famous guitar shop on West 48th Street. (Sadly they closed in 2009 after 74 years of trade). I felt like I was in heaven there.

I must tell you that Patrick has since gone on to be one of the most respected and successful lighting designers in the business and apart from a myriad of concerts and shows for the best in the business, he has worked on performances at the White House for President Obama, Buckingham Palace for Her Majesty The Queen and the opening and closing ceremonies of the 2012 London Olympics… for the world. He was awarded an OBE in the 2014 Birthday Honours List.

Anyway, I was back in London in the spring of 1977 and looking for work. Although the tour had been great in many ways, I decided I would never be a guitar tech again. I was a musician and needed to play. By this time Rod had his own record label, Riva Records, which was named after the 'Italian cigarette speed boat'. There was a publishing company associated with the label that was run by Irishman Billy Gaff, who was Rod's manager at that time. Strangely enough, they were situated at the corner of Waterford Road in Fulham, just a few steps down the street from number 54, which had belonged to my grandmother and where I lived for a while with Jake. It wasn't long before I was offered a songwriting deal with them.

But, not long after signing the agreement Billy called and told me he had signed a new group to his company and told me that they would be opening up for Rod's first tour of North America, sans Faces. Australian musician Russell Hitchcock, and Brit Graham Russell met in May 1975 while performing in the Australian production of *Jesus Christ Superstar* and they formed a group in Melbourne, while the show was still playing. The band was called Air Supply. I was asked to join the band and naturally I jumped at the chance.

So, early summer I was back in LA, where I wanted to be, and feeling quite at home rehearsing with Air Supply or 'Air Wick' as I called them. We embarked on a tour in the summer of 1977, opening for Rod Stewart. This was my first US tour, which was very exciting and great fun. I had lots of friends on the road with me. I remember Rod often sitting in front of the stage whilst we were doing our sound check. Later on he told me he was just checking me out as a guitar player. I had no idea what that meant at the time or how much that would change my life. I do remember that his band knew exactly the timing of when I was about to play an extended solo and would all stand on the side of the stage, whooping and hollering and waving. As soon as I finished the solo, they would leave, which inevitably pissed off the rest of Air Supply! Incidentally, there was one review I recall – obviously written by a very jaded journalist, who basically wrote, 'The Rod Stewart group was awful, and as for Air Supply, it should be cut off!'

The tour went on until almost Christmas and I was very much looking forward to returning home to Eardley Crescent. The British Airways flight back from LA to London on 22nd December 1977 was interesting to say the least. There was much… shall I say… 'tomfoolery'. We had 'a party' in first class, there was much drinking and defacing of passports as some of the members slept. Rod was still glugging a glass of cognac and singing 'Mammy' as we approached the baggage section. I remember Jimmy Horowitz (a manager in the Riva Organisation) riding the carousel while we were waiting for our luggage. He was arrested of course, but was only given a slap on the wrist and a fine. Jim Cregan seemed to have his face smeared with honey and the rest of the band and crew were in various states of dishevelment and ruin.

To our horror, the next day in the press there were photos of the first class cabin that looked like it had been completely taken apart and covered in a coating of foodstuff and drink. Now, we all know that all glasses, bottles, plates, cutlery etc always have to be stowed before landing. So, I reckon some devious journalists, trying to create some scandalous copy, had obviously managed to get on the plane and make a complete mess of the place. I swear that it didn't look like that when we disembarked. Well that's my story and I'm sticking to it.

My grandmother Mary wasn't too pleased at what she saw in the press but I told her it was a 'set up'. Christmas came and went with the usual crowd and a jolly good time was had by all. Although I felt something was missing in my life. That being America. After the tour finished I was asked to stay with the band, but they were based in Australia and I would have to have moved there which I wasn't prepared to do. Los Angeles was now going to be my home.

My love life was looking up during this period. I had met Sharon Arden, now Sharon Osbourne at the Rainbow Bar and Grill on Sunset Strip, and had enjoyed a short lived fling with her. I was very fond of her… still am in fact. Sharon's crooner father Don Arden ran JET records and had managed The Small Faces in the 1960s. Sharon worked for her father and she started going out with Ozzy Osbourne when Don managed Black Sabbath. Don was renowned for not paying his bands properly and he once asked Ian Mclaglan, keyboard player with The

Small Faces, 'What's cooking?' Ian replied, 'Nothing. No money. No food.'

Steve Humphries and I were invited to a big birthday party for Sharon. It was held at the house that she shared with her dad – a sprawling mansion at the top of Tower Drive, just off Benedict Canyon in Beverly Hills. Don was definitely not someone to mess with and had quite a reputation, but having said that I got on with him pretty well. I remember machine gun toting guards at the gate, which seemed a little overbearing. But once inside the house it was nothing but fun. I met Tony Curtis, who was dressed in a dazzling white suit and very entertaining company. And I seem to recall Diana Dors being there too.

Sharon's birthday presents were placed on an exceptionally large table and one large package seemed to be moving. There was no denying it – there was something alive in the box under the wrapping paper. It caused quite a stir when people started to gather around to watch Sharon open her gifts. We hoped it wasn't some small animal or unfortunate pet that had been gift wrapped in Sharon's honour. Sharon thankfully decided to open it first and fell about laughing – as we all did when… a large motorized Dildo squirmed and undulated around the table. Once the hilarity had died down all eyes in the room turned to Sharon's dad – there was certainly some nervousness that the fearsome Don Arden would take umbrage. But, in fact, he wasn't upset about it at all and enjoyed the joke – even if it was at Sharon's expense.

At that time, I was also introduced to a girl by Hamish McAlpine (of the building firm family now a movie producer) who was known by the name of 'LK', short for her real name of Lady Katherine Lambert. We hit it off immediately and we became lovers and great friends. LK was special. Gorgeous. A beautiful tall brunette and ever so seductive. She was very adventurous and liked to dress up as a nurse, which was very exciting once I'd got *Carry On Matron* out of my mind. I was crazy about her although we had a somewhat tempestuous affair. The relationship ended when I got a call from Rikki Farr.

5

SOMEONE TO WATCH OVER ME

June 1978.

I've got to be about the worst letter writer in the world and it's your misfortune that I happen to be your Ma. Kim seems to be very excited about his new group – they have a concert at Ally Pally on 21ˢᵗ July and everyone seems to think it will lead to great things – wouldn't that be marvellous? It's about time something exciting happened for him... I'm lighting a candle to that! It's just what Kim needs at this point in his life I think.

I'm sure you'll be sorry to hear that Guy The Gorilla at London zoo died last week – he was having some teeth removed by gas and had a heart attack. If the public hadn't fed him on pear drops and sherbet dabs he wouldn't have needed his teeth done – sad, isn't it?

Darling I'm so happy about you isn't it marvellous that you are doing what you want – where and with the people you like – not many can say the same – I do wish you everything that's good... go on having a lovely time – I miss you like hell but when I know how well things are going for you it's worth it.

Rikki Farr, who had supplied the sound and lights for the previous tour with Rod and Air Supply, also managed a group in LA called Lion. Rikki was quite a character. Apart from promoting and managing bands, Rikki had put on the Isle of Wight festivals and ran a sound company and Steve Webb, Lion's guitarist, aptly described him as 'The world's guest – everyone loved him even as he hugged you with one arm and nicked the money from your back pocket with the other.' (In 2008, Rikki was jailed in Arizona having pleaded guilty for evading the payment of hundreds of thousands of dollars in tax).

Anyway, back then, Rikki's younger brother Gary Farr was the singer in Lion. Gary was in a quite a famous rhythm and blues band, Gary Farr and the T-Bones, who were a big influence on the London scene group in the early sixties. They were once actually billed as 'Gary Fart and the bones'. We never let him forget that! They had a very famous father – the boxer Tommy Farr, who was considered one of the greatest ever British heavyweights – he even went the distance with the legendary Joe Louis. Lion were now were looking for another guitarist and good old Patrick Woodroffe had suggested me. The band was signed to a very famous label, A & M records, which was run by Herb Alpert and Gerry Moss. Rikki wanted me to come to LA to try out for the gig and he told me that if it worked out I would have to move there. I told him, 'I'll be there tomorrow.'

So when I had to tell my girlfriend 'LK' that I had the opportunity to go to LA to join Lion she said, 'I'll never see you again.' 'Of course you will,' I replied. 'I'm sure I'll be back in a week or so.' I knew I was just trying to be gentle but in my heart of hearts I knew she was right. After I went to live in LA, we wrote each other for some months. Then I didn't hear from her for a while – she had found someone else. I never did see her again.

I flew to LAX on 22nd May 1978 and was met by Steve Webb. He recalls, 'When I picked Robin up from LA and drove him to Topanga he was very quiet and justifiably tired after a long flight and man he had a lot of guitars with him! As the other guitarist I was tasked with showing him how the tunes went and he was very quick to pick them up. We had a rehearsal and it clicked right away. Everyone was happy with him and he had a similar sense of humour to the rest of us. Robin brought a good solid rock 'n' roll feel to the band and as we worked out the sometimes very complex parts, it was soon apparent that the added power was right on the money. Robin has a unique way of playing crunchy rock n roll rhythms and it felt like he'd always been in the band. Our vocalist,

Gary Farr asked him, probably quite soon after the first run through, if he was interested in being in Lion. Robin replied, "Does a bear shit in the woods?!" And that was it. Problem solved.'

Lion. Left to right – Steve Humphries, Garry Farr, me,
Steve Webb, John Sinclair and Eric Dillon (STEVE WEBB)

It was true. Within five minutes of 'the audition' I thought I had got the gig. I was very happy as they seemed not only a fine bunch of musicians but also lovely guys and we got on like a house on fire from the very beginning. Also in the band were Steve Humphries (Bass), Eric Dillon (drums), and John Sinclair (keyboards).

I moved in with Gary and Steve Webb in what was called an 'A' framed house at 22012 Old Topanga School Road. Right in the centre of Topanga Canyon about a half hour drive from Hollywood. It was then and is, still to this day, a kind of hippie community with all sorts of weird and odd people living there. A real 60s vibe, lots of tie dye and VW campers. There was a deck around the house and we would stand there in T-shirt and shorts with our Fender Strats plugged into little battery powered amps which had a volume and 'on' switch shaped like a pig's nose and was obviously called a 'Pignose'.

The house had a rehearsal/recording studio on the ground floor which was perfect as we didn't have to rent anywhere to rehearse or record. We were given $120 a week, which in those days just about covered our daily expenses, i.e. wine, food and of course cigarettes in my case. I remember a pack of Winston was $1.50. Funnily enough Winston is still my brand (Is this what you call product placement?). I was given Gary's spare car, a chocolate brown Mercury Bobcat – one of the most dangerous cars on the road then. The vehicle was immediately re-christened 'Bograt' by John Sinclair who also had one. The fuel tank was in the back and they would catch fire if rear ended. But it never happened to me. I was lucky, very lucky! Just up the road was a dive called The Corral, where we used to play quite often. There were a lot of rehearsals and much imbibing of Janis Joplin's favourite tipple, Southern Comfort.

Soon after I joined the band, Steve Webb and I went to the Rainbow Bar and Grill that night to celebrate. The Rainbow is legendary – probably the oldest and most notorious restaurant/bar in LA and always filled with friends and associates in the music business. We took off down Sunset, looking for a canyon to head over the Hollywood hills to the freeway out to Topanga. I was driving pretty fast and I missed my turn. I screeched round the corner and within seconds, lights started flashing behind us and we were pulled over by a black and white police car. Not only was I speeding, a little worse for wear, but in the back seat there was a fancy fold up chair marked with a Calabasas restaurant logo I had earlier appropriated.

The traffic cop produced a large notepad. I jokingly ordered a Big Mac and fries. He didn't laugh.

He asked me, 'You're in a hurry, what's up?'

I told him I was a bit lost and hadn't long arrived from England.

Do you know how fast you were going?'

'Yes I do.'

'And do you know the shortcut across Coldwater Canyon to the Ventura Freeway to Topanga?'

'Yes I do.'

'Then, take it.'

I was amazed that he didn't breathalyse me or even question me about how much I had imbibed. So I drove off... very slowly. To this day, Steve is convinced that it was my accent that saved the day and I probably did go a bit Terry-Thomas on the cop.

While in Topanga, I received quite a lot of letters from the family and in one early missive, Joannie wrote, 'Dad is in great form making a Walt Disney movie (*The Spaceman and King Arthur*) with Kenneth More up in Newcastle. The enclosed picture shows him in knightly garb on the Royal Podium, and what do you think he's clasping in his fingers? Not an ordinary cigarette! Forsooth...'

It reminded me that I once accompanied Dad to a BAFTA awards dinner. Princess Anne was sitting at the next table and Dad whispered to me, 'Do you have one of *those* cigarettes?' So I rolled him a joint which he duly smoked. We didn't offer the Princess a toke... I'm not sure she would have been amused.

At another BAFTA awards ceremony in 1972, Dad was nominated for his appearance in *Traitor*, a BBC drama written by Dennis Potter in which he played the part of a British defector Adrian Harris, a character loosely based on the infamous double agent Kim Philby. This was quite a departure for Dad, who was quoted as saying he was 'very, very scared that he wouldn't be able to pull it off.' Of course he did and, in fact, the critics were full of praise for his performance.

The ceremony was at the Royal Albert Hall and Mum, Jake and I were glued to the television set at home, hoping and praying that he would win the BAFTA. When his name was announced and he went up to receive the award from Annette Crosby, we were all in tears. I would have loved to have been with him as would Mum. She was delighted that Dad was finally being recognised by his peers for his acting talent, but was also upset that she wasn't with him and part of the celebrations.

My dad also wrote to me in June 1978 – a typically encouraging missive from him:

Darling Robin,
I am so pleased you are settling down with the group. I do hope all goes well for you I really think you are doing awfully well...
I expect you are preparing the Album session as I write this.

The album he was referring to was a project that we shared that year. Working with Dad was something I'd always wanted to do. Musician

69

and composer Mike Gill, who was employed by Riva Records, was always a great believer in me and it was he who had the idea about Dad and I making a record of *The Velveteen Rabbit*, a wonderful children's book by Margery Williams about a toy rabbit coming to life through the love from the little boy who owned it. After a lot of negotiation with the record company, we recorded the album, which was produced by a guy called Stuart Taylor. I had always enjoyed the charming book and the idea was that I would play guitar and Dad would narrate the text. Ed Welch wrote most of the music and I also wrote some pieces for guitar. It was an experience that we would both always treasure. I recorded my parts in LA while Dad did his work in London. The record was very touching and kids absolutely loved it. Joannie used to put it on to entertain friends' children when they came around. Dad was quoted in the *Daily Express* as saying, 'We got on wonderfully well, I've always treated the boys as friends… they were the kind of people who are not motivated for eagerness for fame. We just want satisfying work and survival.'

Sorry I've gone off at a tangent (again). So… anyway… after a few months of rehearsing and recording at the house in Topanga Canyon, most of the Lion band members had to go back to England to get H1 visas to allow us to continue working in the States. They could last anywhere from six months to a year. We were being 'sponsored 'by A & M so it wouldn't be difficult. In fact, if we hadn't been signed to them we would have stayed in the US. We returned to London. Steve Humphries and I stayed with Mum at Eardley Crescent and John Sinclair stayed with his own mum!

We were home for about a week or so, sorting out our visas but also enjoying a kind of a short break. I remember one night we all went to an Indian restaurant near where John's mum lived near Hammersmith. We had a great meal and chose Indian food, as at that time in LA, there was only one Indian restaurant, situated in Westwood and very expensive for what it was. During the meal, some guy came in, obviously three sheets to the wind, ordered various items from the menu slurring and cursing at the waiter. He was 'effing and blinding' and drinking more and more lager. He continued swearing at the staff and became more and more abusive. We asked our waiter, 'How can you put up with his diabolical behaviour?' To which he replied, 'He's a very good customer.'

We all cracked up, but unfortunately it was what they had to put up in those days… and no doubt still do.

After about a week at Eardley Crescent, it was time to get back to my 'new home' in LA. We had an early departure the next morning so I said my goodbyes to my grandmother, Mary, the night before. Mum and Jake were at the front door as we got in the car to take us to Heathrow. After I got back to California, I called Mum to tell her we were safe and sound. She told me that just after we left, Mary had climbed the stairs to say goodbye again but just missed us by seconds. She told Mum, 'That's the last time I'll see Robin.'

In February 1979 Mum made her daily telephone call to Mary at her home in Waterford Road, only to be told that grandma wasn't feeling well. Mum went over immediately but soon after she arrived, Mary collapsed and literally died in Mum's arms, having suffered a pulmonary embolism. I adored Mary, who was incredibly warm and affectionate and much loved by all who knew her. Mum had always been absolutely devoted to her mother and was naturally distraught. I don't think she ever came to terms with her mother's death.

Lion were now ready to record and we needed a producer. Steve Webb has written about the audition process, 'We saw Roy Thomas Baker, who came out in a Rolls and a fur coat, the temperature was 30°C, he listened and said, "You want stringy-poohs do you?" Gary wasn't having that. Todd Rundgren, who sat on the floor and trashed the lyrics, said if he took the job it would end up a Todd album, Gary wasn't having that. Glyn Johns (Stones etc.), after a listen, said he'd take the synth outside and chop it up first thing. Finally Ron Nevison came out, said nothing, just told us to play and recorded us using our 8 track and ropey old mixer. The result was stunning compared to our own efforts up to then and we wanted him on the case immediately.'

It was true. Ron, an old pal of Steve Humphries, totally blew us away and managed to get great sounds out of our little gear – sounds we had never been able to get ourselves. Ron had engineered some Led Zeppelin material and had huge hits in the States with The Babys and other acts.

We laid down Lion's first album at the famous Record Plant on 3rd Street, near La Cienega Boulevard in the heart of LA. Previous artistes who had recorded there included Alice Cooper, Sly Stone and Todd

Rundgren. It all went swimmingly well and we were all happy with the result... until there was a spanner thrown into the works. Rikki and Ron had a great falling out over the art direction for the cover. They had such an argument that Rikki decided not to release the album and so we had to re-record it all again – this time with the Grammy winning Pete Henderson at the helm, Supertramp's producer at the time.

We weren't happy with the results of the new tracks as it was almost impossible to recreate the first recording. I've sometimes thought that a demo sounds much better than the actual release, which can lose the spontaneity and spirit of the original recording. I've often wondered, 'why are we doing this again?' Ask any musician about trying to better even a very good demo. That version was released but it was nothing like the original.

Any possible profit for A&M's was lost because the recording debacle. We were now on weekly pay of about $200 – not exactly a huge amount, but the studio costs and the equipment mounted up. The new recording didn't do all that well and we were dropped by the label.

Rikki also managed The Tubes, a San Francisco based band with a very loyal following. Lion opened up for them and Bernie Boyle was our tour manager (Bernie has since toured with the likes of Michael Jackson, Paul McCartney and Faith Hill).

After some time it became obvious that Lion had musical differences with Gary so we decided we would be more cohesive without him. He took it quite well and he joined a band called Jumping Dogs which included Fred Tackett from Little Feat. Gary later became a stills photographer on Hollywood films until his premature death at the age of fifty from a heart attack – after a particularly strenuous bicycle ride, a hobby he had taken up in Topanga.

I lived in Topanga for about six months. It was quite a drive to and from the various venues – sometimes twice a day – and so I moved more centrally to an apartment on Hawthorn Avenue, in the midst of Hollywood. Around this time I was having terrible stomach ache and really bad heartburn. At the end of November I went to see a doctor and underwent a full medical. I was declared in good health apart from having an ulcer. He explained to me that it wasn't too bad but I had to change my diet drastically for a month; no tea, coffee and no spicy food. The final catastrophe was, 'You can't drink.' The regimen just happened to come to an end on 31st December. And there just happened to be a New Years Eve party at Le Dôme restaurant on Sunset Strip, owned by Eddie Kerkhofs.

Needless to say I made up for not drinking for a month. It was a fabulous party with lots of friends there. I returned home in the wee hours. At about eight the next morning, I woke up very suddenly, feeling disorientated. Shaking from too much vodka maybe? Was the previous night's culinary indulgence making me feel nauseous? No, I had woken up with a shock. Literally. There had actually been a small earthquake moments before and what with the hangover, I experienced quite a wake-up call. Perhaps it was my punishment and I had suffered 'God's wrath'. The earthquake was all my fault!

Eddie Kerkhofs is an old friend of mine and has a very interesting background. Born in Belgium he served his apprenticeship as a chef in France. He came to the States and worked in Boston before borrowing the airfare to come to LA in 1969. He took the bus from LAX to the corner of Hollywood and Vine because 'that's what you did'. He found employment as a waiter at Au Petit Café, which was the first French restaurant in Hollywood and was frequented by Sergio Mendes and Herb Alpert.

Eddie then became manager at 'St Germaine' restaurant and was introduced to the music world as there were lots of record companies such as Motown, Capital and Atlantic based around Sunset Strip. Los Angeles, funnily enough, wasn't a late night city and at that time, the chef would only work until 10pm whereas the musicians would only arrive after 11pm and were actually more concerned with drinking rather than eating. Eddie realised that there was a chance to fill the gap and he and a chef friend decided to open their own restaurant on Sunset Strip. The found a location which was then an office block and in a very dodgy neighbourhood. They needed to borrow $800,000 from a bank to build and open the restaurant and Eddie managed to obtain sponsors to invest in the restaurant – including Ringo Starr and Bernie Taupin and in return each would receive thousands of dollars worth of food and drink. Le Dôme had a 'Black Tie' opening in 1975 and immediately became the talk of the town.

This was the only place in town that stayed open until 1am. Then the front door was closed allowing back door entry until all hours. What we would now call a 'lockdown.' Artists arrived at Le Dôme after the concerts had finished and sometimes didn't get there until 12.30am. It was a great place to hang out. Even if you just wanted a drink, you were guaranteed to find someone you knew. Apparently Tom Jones was often at the restaurant until 7am and Eddie had to pay the chefs overtime just in case the musicians wanted something to eat in the middle of the night. For a number of years it was the hottest place to lunch. Movie executives would hold power lunches and would reserve and pay for adjacent tables simply so that that they wouldn't be overheard.

We'll always have Paris. With Eddie Kerkhofs and his wife, Britt.

Meanwhile, there had been another, much more significant event and change to my life – personal not professional. One night in 1978 as I was hanging out at the Rainbow I got talking to a beautiful girl. I joined her at her table as she just happened to be sitting next to someone I knew. Confusingly, she was called Robin, but unlike me, she was a 'Bunny' at the Playboy club in Century City. We had a drink and within a few minutes of meeting her I said to her, 'I'm going to marry you.' I'd never been so presumptuous before, but I was absolutely convinced that she was 'Miss Right'. I also discovered to my astonishment that Robin had a sister called Kim. An extraordinary coincidence – we were both called Robin and both with siblings called Kim.

Robin was naturally a bit taken aback at the impetuousness of my marriage declaration, but not completely put off, as we started going out straightaway and began living together in an apartment near Universal Studios just a month or two after our first meeting. 'Bun' (we started to call her 'Bun' to avoid confusion) had actually been living with a violinist, Nick, in England. They were going to get married, but broke up and the immigration officials wouldn't let her remain in England. She had only been back in LA for a fortnight when we met, so the timing was perfect for us both. Bun and I moved to a house near the Hollywood Bowl and I used to drive her to work at the Playboy Club in Century City every day. We really loved that house, were very happy and had some great times together. I knew so many ex-pats living in LA and Bun was such an anglophile that she felt so comfortable with all 'the Brits'.

Back in London, Jake was still living at Eardley Crescent and occupied the basement flat which was a haven for his friends and hangers-on. Mum occupied the first floor and kept the ground floor as somewhere where visiting pals could stay. I know now that, at the time, there was some concern from Mum's friends that Jake took her for granted – there was nothing that she wouldn't do for him. I'm not surprised – it wasn't just Mum and Dad that found Jake lovable. He was bright and funny and had an amazing effect on nearly everyone he met. But Mum had always worried about Jake, as exhibited in this letter from her to me from the Adelphi Hotel, Liverpool on 17th August 1978.

I am here in Liverpool doing a photographic session for selling somebody's Christmas hampers – I've only got to see a string

*of tinsel and a jar of mincemeat and I get quite sentimental…
we will have Christmas day on Sunday and of course the house
will be open and full of food etc. Do you really think you'll be
able to make it darling – I am so frightened that they won't let
you into the country again… you are very much missed and we
all have to tell ourselves that at least you are doing what you
want to do and loving it and that makes us feel much better…
Central Line (Jake's band) doesn't seem to have taken off yet
although they are still working very hard and I just loved the
tape I heard – written by Kim – that came as a surprise to me.
'The Demon' doesn't seem to have got himself together yet –
still helping himself to things and the phone bills for the last
two quarters have been about £500 more than they should have
been – calls to Amsterdam and now USA – I don't know what
to do about him, I get so worried sometimes – I only long for
him to make it with his band, maybe that will help him to get
himself straightened out.*

Mum continued to worry about Jake, who she actually never called
'Jake', although I'm not sure she was ever quite aware of the seriousness
of his drug problem. He was, at least, working more and the following
year she wrote to me with more encouraging news that Jake was
supporting Roy Ayers on his English tour and that 'the band have been
put on salary and it's made such a difference to Kimbo – I am so pleased
for him. He is playing two dates upstairs at Ronnie Scott's – so that's
good isn't it'?

Mum was very unwell during the summer of 1980. She was open
about how much she missed her own mother. She had confided to
friends that she felt she wasn't going to be around for very much longer,
but hadn't told me – no doubt she was trying to protect me. In June,
I rang mum and told her that I was planning to get married to Bun
in England in October. Her response was surprising; 'No, get married
now.' She was pleased for me but adamant that I should bring forward
the wedding. On reflection, this was, of course somewhat ominous
and I should have guessed something was wrong. Mum was obviously
convinced that her health was failing fast and felt that she wasn't going
to be around for much longer.

So I did as she asked and Bun and I were married in August of 1980. We chose the Little Brown Church, a historic (for California) chapel on Coldwater Canyon, Studio City, made famous by the marriage of Ronald and Nancy Reagan in the 1950s. The preacher at the wedding's father was reputed to be an underground gang boss, which made the venue even more interesting.

It was a small intimate affair. My best man was Matt Leach, who used to work for our manager, Rikki Farr and Bun's maid of honour was Michelle Dobbs, whose tour manager husband Steve, worked for Elton John. John Sinclair played the piano and everyone was dressed to the nines. Fat Mattress drummer Eric Dillon even wore a tuxedo T-shirt. There was inevitably much amusement when the priest said, 'Do you, Robin, take Robin… and do you, Robin, take Robin… etc etc?'

Afterwards the reception was held at the Beachwood Canyon home of our friends Steve and Anita Webb. It was a lot of fun with much booze on hand and Bun's mum made a huge cake by spreading gallons of Crisco shortening onto a huge square of polystyrene foam and then covering the pastry with icing to create a very unusual base… and all with a fag in her mouth. Glenn Hughes, later to be a band member of Deep Purple, entertained us all night. A wonderful singer. And I do mean all night! I recall it was difficult getting him to go home. He used to have drug and alcohol problems but, I'm pleased to say, has now been sober for over twenty years.

I wasn't making much money then and Bun was working at Playboy, Mum was helping out financially, sending us cheques whenever she could. In the last weekend of September she hosted a particularly lively lunch party at Eardley Crescent in the company of Bruce Copp, Joan Sims and actor Nigel Hamilton. Nigel later wrote, 'It was a magical occasion. Hattie was on top form. It was almost as if she realised that she was very ill and was determined to enjoy herself even more than ever.'

Mum's weight had ballooned even more and she was very breathless. She was admitted briefly to Charing Cross hospital at the beginning of October, but persuaded the medical staff to let her come home for the weekend because she was due to attend a charity event. She developed chest pains but refused to call a doctor. She also had a heated argument with Jake before she went to bed – something that haunted Jake for the rest of his life. By mid morning the following day, Mum had not been seen. Jake took her in a cup of tea in bed, but found her dead. She had tragically passed away during the night.

Jake rang Dad, who tried to telephone me in Los Angeles but couldn't get hold of me and so left a message with Rod Stewart's manager, Billy Gaff, who later broke the awful news. It was quite early in the morning and I was still asleep. I really don't remember what Billy said as I was still groggy from sleep. What I do remember is being told she died in her sleep due to a massive heart attack. I felt as if something had been torn out of me. She was irreplaceable and as she was relatively young, I felt robbed. It was a huge loss. And even more difficult because I was so far away in Los Angeles. I didn't really know how to cope with the situation. I realised that my mother's health had been deteriorating dramatically for some time and she was quite open with me that her body, which she had always resented for aesthetic reasons, was now failing her physically. She had told me that she'd had enough. I think she died because she couldn't take any more, she was tired and fed up with her health and wanted to move on. I was heartbroken.

Bun and I realised we had to get to London as quickly as possible. We managed to get a flight a couple of days later and were soon in London at Eardley Crescent. I remember getting a phone call from a journalist a day or so after we got to London. He told me that he'd done a lot of research about Mum but couldn't find anything that put her in a bad light. I didn't quite know how to respond and he continued, 'Well I just thought I'd tell you – so I'm writing something positive about her.' 'Unbelievable cheek,' I thought.

Obituaries appeared in most of the national newspapers the day after her death. *The Daily Telegraph* stated that, 'Hattie Jacques was a leading popular entertainer for more than 30 years and a versatile actress of great accomplishment' and *The Times'* columnist wrote, 'Hattie Jacques will be remembered with affection by all who saw her in a clutch of *Carry On* films; heard her on the radio; and never missed her appearance with Eric Sykes… she was a very accomplished comedian.' Unfortunately – but somewhat predictably – *The Sun* couldn't resist describing her as, 'The roly-poly, fifteen stone comedy star'.

There were so many tributes from friends and fellow thespians and

Dad stated, 'We have lost a very remarkable lady. I feel very shocked and full of grief. She had a wealth of talent which was often underestimated. Some people are dim witted at times. They see a large lady and can't see further. She always showed tremendous generosity and kindness to other people and was a great giver of thought and help.'

An edition of *The Times,* on 8th October 1980, under the headline, 'NO INQUEST ON ACTRESS' reported that, 'Hattie Jacques, the actress, who was found dead at her home in Earl's Court, London, Monday, died from a heart attack, a post mortem examination confirmed yesterday.'

We stayed in London for two weeks and it rained every single day except the day of Mum's funeral, which was cold but gloriously sunny. The funeral took place at Putney Vale Crematorium. She had never participated in any organised religion and didn't attend church, but she did believe in God. The service was actually quite simple and there wasn't even a eulogy from the Minister. There was a selection of some her favourite songs, including 'Someone To Watch Over Me'. Mum had issued specific instructions in advance, requesting no flowers, instead asking for donations to be made to her favourite charities. She also wanted everyone to enjoy a party afterwards – with no tears. That was impossible for all of us. As Joannie later wrote, 'She might as well have asked the Thames to stop flowing.'

At home in LA, I am surrounded by many family photographs scattered around our apartment in West Hollywood. Mum was great in *Hancock* and the *Carry On* movies and she shone in the *Sykes* television series. Everyone loved her for that – and I think *Dad's Army* is still hysterically funny. The fact that all those shows are still so popular is a great tribute to my parents. It was sad that Bun never met Mum in person although they spoke regularly on the telephone and Bun always said it felt like she'd known Mum all her life; 'When I was hyper, she would calm me right down. She made me feel like I was part of the family straightaway and she was always so happy for us and about us. I really felt robbed when she died… her arms were wrapped around me I felt completely at peace with her.'

Mum had that affect on everyone.

Martin Christopherson, who had become one of Mum's closest confidantes, was the executor of her will. He put the house at Eardley

Crescent, the family home, up for sale almost immediately and underpriced at £80,000 it was sold very quickly. Quite a few valuable antique pieces mysteriously disappeared from the house before it was sold and the general feeling was that Christopherson was responsible. Jake and I were very upset at the speed of events. It wasn't just about the money – this was the house that we had grown up in and which held so many happy memories. Christopherson told us it needed to be sold quickly to pay for death duties Mum and my grandmother had accrued. It was awful that I had no say in any of these events whatever, as I was in LA at the time. I would have loved to have kept that place. And sadly, in years to come, this once lovely Victorian house was subsequently divided into about twelve tiny flats.

A Comic Heritage blue plaque in Hattie's honour was added to the exterior of the house – the first for a comedy actress. Joannie attended the ceremony and was able to visit the house for the first time in fifteen years. She recalls, 'Eardley Crescent passed into the hands of somebody who sliced all the grand and airy rooms into little plywood units and crammed it full. The lovely living-room where so many wonderful Christmas parties had taken place was now half its size, the beautiful marble fireplace was gone and the soul of the house had fled. Even the hall was now narrowed to two grim tunnels, one leading upstairs and one down to the basement flat.' The house has now been divided into over fifteen flats and bed sitting rooms.

Unfortunately Lion had fallen apart that same year, so we moved on, changing the name of the group to The Difference. Our style had changed too as we became much more rock 'n' roll and began to get quite a good following. Steve Webb recalls, 'There was a tremendous energy and commitment from everyone. We launched the band on LA, aiming to play every club and pick up a following. We painted all the gear red, white and blue, not an original idea we knew, but it looked great! Keyboards, amps, monitors, a white drum kit! And we plastered posters all the way up and down the canyon drives into Hollywood advertising every gig. The record company folk couldn't miss us! We had custom envelopes, pins, and even a Difference invoice which was sent to all the key label folk for every important gig.'

We played all the gigs around LA in legendary venues including, Blue Lagoon, The Central, the Whisky a Go Go and The Troubadour. A review by Bruce Duff, in *Music Connection* of one of our Troubadour gigs stated, 'Pop music melodically similar to the slickness of McCartney or even Billy Joel packed inside intricate "progressive" arrangements… the positive effect of this is the resulting variety of textures, dynamics, instrumental riffs and ensemble parts which keeps the listener engulfed in an unending series of ideas, or songs within songs… the musicianship is top notch. Both Steve Webb and Robin Le Mesurier are more than adequate string benders, John Sinclair plays magnificently. Webb also possesses one of those great rock-pop voices.' Matt Leach was Rikki Farr's 'second in command' in Lion and now looked after The Difference. At one time Matt was Raquel Welch's tour manager and brought her to one of the shows at The Corral. So I invited Britt Ekland to the same gig… as you do… I can't begin to describe the jaw dropping and gaping at those two beauties as they entered the venue. It was a fun show. Almost every Sunday I would go to Britt's house for dinner. She lived not far from me on Stone Canyon Road. That's where I first met Victoria Sellers, Peter and Britt's daughter, who was then a very young girl.

We also gigged at Madame Wong's. Madame Wong wasn't just the name of a club. She actually existed! The formidable Esther Wong had been born in Shanghai, but had emigrated to the US in 1949 and became a music promoter having established a restaurant with a floorshow in Chinatown. She was later dubbed the Godmother of Punk, although that moniker has inevitably since been disputed.

We actually got ourselves banned from Madame Wong's by Madame Wong herself. While Steve Humphries distracted her in conversation – Steve was good at being a good looking, chirpy cockney – I dodged behind the bar and purloined a crate of beer, which I was trying to transport to the dressing room. I tried to carry it behind my back, which wasn't easy because it weighed a ton. Anyhow I must have been struggling and the clinking of the bottles alerted Madame Wong to my miscreant behaviour. She erupted with anger and screamed at me, forcing me to return the beer to its rightful place. That, I believe, was the last time we played at the club!

Steve Webb has since written, 'We had girlfriends, wives and friends helping to publicise the band with flyers and a lawyer friend, who kept us informed of what record labels were looking for, but it was hard to keep up the energy while apparently swimming against the tide. Despite good reviews and the talent and spirit in the band, the clubs didn't really pay enough to sustain us. The unfair reputation that we had gained in spending the A&M money seemed to put off any possible record deals.'

⅂HE
DIFFERENCE

Steve Webb, Steve Humphries, John Sinclair, me and Eric Dillon (STEVE WEBB)

It was during this time, in 1981, that I received a call from Malcolm Culmore asking me if I'd like to do a television show with Rod Stewart – the first American Music Awards Show in Los Angeles, hosted by Dick Clark, which was due to be shot in a few days time. My old mate Pete Buckland, who managed the group, had suggested me – for which I'll always be grateful, when Gary Grainger, who I knew from the days of Stryder dropped out. He had developed a fear of flying and wasn't keen on flying to the States. 'Would I?' was my immediate response. There was no question about it. Here was the opportunity of playing with one of the world's foremost rock singers. It was a great honour and the other advantage was that we'd known each other for years and so I wasn't in the least 'star struck'.

'Passion' was the song on the show. It wasn't a live performance and we mimed to playback. I think we shot the song a couple of times. Most of the conversations were about what should we wear – still is, as a matter of fact, for TV recordings! The only other artist I remember on that shoot was Crystal Gayle who had a huge hit at the time with 'Don't It Make My Brown Eyes Blue'.

Sometimes you just have to be in the right place at the right time. Plus a modicum of luck. The television show had gone well and I must have fitted into the band because a couple of days afterwards, I was asked to join The Rod Stewart Group as a permanent member. I was still with The Difference and I always felt a little guilty about this, but it was an opportunity that I just couldn't refuse – the band was struggling and the guys understood. John Sinclair, who joined Uriah Heep and then worked with Ozzy Osbourne for a number of years, recalls that I was very apologetic, 'I don't believe any of us felt anything other than disappointment at losing him. We had to wish him all the best as gigs like that don't turn up every day and I'm sure I would have done the same given the chance. In fact I know I would!' Eric became an airline pilot, Steve Humphries opened a pub – The Cat and Fiddle – on Sunset Boulevard and Steve Webb carried on touring, doing session work and writing… and continues to do so very successfully.

Rod's band at that time consisted of Jim Cregan, Danny Johnson (guitars), Kevin Savigar (keyboards), Carmine Appice (drums), Jay Davis (bass) and Rod of course. I was introduced to the multi talented and subsequently award laden Kevin Savigar by Jim Cregan at the Rainbow, where we shared a few beers. I then invited him to Sunday dinner and we became fast friends. Kevin later moved to Los Angeles and joined the quarter of a million Brits living in LA at the time.

Rod and I also got on well right from the start, sharing a similar sense of humour and he is now is one of my best mates. He has a great sense of humour and is a huge Tony Hancock fan – given that my mum worked with the great comedian in *Hancock's Half Hour* it was inevitable that we would get on – never mind the music.

We used to rehearse in Rod's garage at his house on Carolwood Drive in Holmby Hills. He lived next door to the iconic Hollywood actor Gregory Peck, who was lovely and quite happy to listen to the band blasting out the music. Other neighbours were a bit put out by the band's presence and the rehearsal noise, but Gregory was incredibly encouraging, said he enjoyed having them around and actually came to listen to us rehearse. 'I like Rod's music,' were his exact words. He and his wife even cut a hole in the fence so that some of us could use their tennis court.

It was at this time that Rod decided we needed a sax player. I told him that I knew someone, Jimmy Zavala, who was not only great on reeds, but also a brilliant harmonica player too. He was married to one of the girls that worked with Bun when she was at The Playboy Club and we had hung out together. We tried Jimmy out and he became the eighth member of the group.

There was a tour of Japan due to start in a couple of months, so after we finished basic rehearsals at Rod's house, we went into full production rehearsals on a sound stage somewhere in LA at Paramount studios, I think... or it could have been the pub round the corner. Doesn't really matter, I suppose...

The tour of Japan was very successful and we all had much fun on and off stage. The audiences over there are, as you might imagine, very reserved. They would go crazy with applause after a song for about ten seconds or so, and then maintain silence. You could hear a pin drop before the next song was introduced. We were used to audiences that got up and danced and so it was odd at first but we got used to it and I suppose they were being very respectful.

There was one particular club in Tokyo called The Lexington Queen, run by an American, Bill Hershey, which we frequented as much as possible. It was a favourite hangout for American and English bands and a host of US models on assignment there. I learned some years later that, on one occasion, they wouldn't let Kenny Rogers into the club. A spokesman for the club was quoted as saying, 'We've had The Rod Stewart Group in here in the past and we have changed our policy.' I didn't think we were that badly behaved. And poor old Kenny Rogers, who had absolutely nothing to do with us, was barred! Each night, on almost every street corner, little soba noodle bars were set up for late night snacking. They really couldn't hold more than a handful of people, but we always managed to get all of us crammed in.

We would often do the 'table creep' – occupying a long table at a restaurant at the end of which would open up to the street. Very slowly, during the meal, we would move the entire table so half of it was on the pavement completely blocking pedestrian traffic. I don't ever remember any of the staff at any of the restaurants ever complaining. Foolish behaviour indeed. There was more foolish behaviour in the form of 'sake madness'. Almost every time we had a night off, of which there were quite a few, we would all have dinner together at which much sake was consumed – some would say too much – but not us.

We used to spike Jim Cregan's sake with vodka and the rest of the guys would pretend to drink as much as him but either filling their glasses with water or surreptitiously emptying the contents of their glasses when he wasn't watching. Jim couldn't understand why he was getting so drunk while the others remained sober. In the end we told him what had been going on. He just looked at us all and said, 'Bastards!' We finally called a truce when he was so smashed that he fell over in the hotel lobby and hurt himself on the marble floor, chipping a bone in his elbow. He begged for mercy and so we stopped spiking his drink. After all, we weren't sadists.

Travelling to another gig in Nagasaki, one evening we were travelling on The Bullet Train from Tokyo. I reckon almost every young boy of my era wanted to be an engine driver and I was no different so I asked our Japanese go-between if I could visit the train controller at the front of the train. She agreed and took me up there. To watch the controller – a figure of intense concentration, staring unblinkingly at the track in front of him and because the train was run by computers, he barely touched any controls. The driver was wearing spotless white gloves and dressed very smartly in sharp black trousers and a crisp white jacket, buttoned at the back. I was so enthralled it must have been five minutes or so before I asked if I could get Rod to join me – he is also a huge train enthusiast.

This request was swiftly agreed and Rod and I spent the rest of the journey at the front of the train taking it all in and being quite astonished at how calm the driver remained while hurtling along the track at such a high speed. The chances of repeating that experience these days is about as slim as sitting in the cockpit of a commercial jet! It was an amazing experience.

Later on, Rod started building his own model railway at his house on Carolwood drive. We would spend hours laying track. After he moved to his house in Beverly Park, he started another model railway, this time on the top floor of the house. His railway has been on the cover and featured in an American magazine called *Model Railroader* a number of times.

The tour was going so well – the music was great and the band all got on famously. However, the happiness of the time was shattered by news from LA. I was relaxing in my hotel bedroom when Billy Francis rushed into see me. Bun had apparently been involved in a terrible car crash in Los Angeles and had been seriously injured. I was distraught and my immediate thoughts were naturally to leave the tour and return home to be with her. After some frantic phone calls I eventually got hold of her. She was in hospital but she told me to stay and finish the tour and it was agreed that we would meet in London when it was over. She was insistent about it so I remained in Japan. But, of course, I was desperate to know what had happened...

Bun was still working at the Playboy club and one evening a friend, the brother of another Bunny offered her a lift to work – he wanted to see his sister at work... and in her Bunny costume (No, I don't know why either and I'm definitely not going there).

Anyway, I had bought Bun a new dress just before I went away which she decided to wear that evening. But as she was getting dressed, she heard a voice in her head, telling her that she was never ever going to wear the dress again. This voice kept repeating that something terrible was going happen and she also saw images of spilt blood. Anyway, the guy arrived to pick her up in his old Dodge Dart and she got in. There wasn't a seat belt and because she felt unsettled, she locked the door.

Five minutes into the journey, a drunk driver smashed into the car and Bun's head went through the windscreen, leaving her trapped in the car. Both drivers were unscathed and tried to get her out but because she had locked the door, they had to drag her out through the windscreen. She was terribly badly hurt. In fact she was unconscious and described a near death experience which lasted about ten minutes and in which she felt incredibly peaceful and calm and ready to relinquish her life. She then she heard my mother's voice telling her, 'You're still together, don't leave us, you have so much life to live.'

The ambulance rushed Bun to hospital where she regained consciousness and hysterically started shouting orders to everybody whilst still in a state of shock. She screamed that she was a Playboy Bunny, her husband was a well known rock musician and she demanded the best plastic surgeon in Los Angeles!

Bun was lucky in the end. They did indeed find one of the best plastic surgeons in California in the shape of the amazing Dr Neal Handel, who just so happened to be a customer at the Playboy Club and actually knew Bun. She later told me that her nose was actually hanging off and she had to have 160 stitches in her face. Poor Bun had also suffered a lot of other physical injuries.

I wanted to return home to LA and join her, but as I've said Bun persuaded me to stay in Japan and finish the tour. I was reluctant, but she was insistent that she was ok and so I agreed.

The tour was actually then extended when Billy Gaff decided we should play a couple more dates and Pete Buckland managed to get two more shows in Hong Kong and Thailand. I remember the descent into Hong Kong being pretty scary. Before the new airport in Hong Kong was built, the descent into the old one was harrowing as the planes had to come down extremely low over the hotchpotch of residences. You could almost see what people were watching on TV before the landing.

When we got to the stadium for the sound check, the stage was built about fifty yards from some of the audience members. We all wondered how long it would be before they move forward to be as close as possible. When it came to the show there was very little security so it was probably during the second song that they all came thundering towards us. It was a bit scary at that moment but luckily they didn't actually manage to ascend the stage. In hindsight the promoter should have thought about them being so far away in the first place.

I've never experienced so much humidity as I did in Bangkok. It was hardly worth blow drying my hair because as soon as I stepped out of the air conditioned hotel and on to the street it was like going into a sauna! I suppose we can't all look fabulous all the time. Ha! We did the usual tourist things whilst we were there, including visiting the snake ranches, having a great lunch on a river boat. That was the first time I was introduced to Thai food, and I loved it. We had a few fun days there before the gig, which was actually promoted by the chief of police (he clearly hadn't heard about my 'Womble' drug bust). It was strange to witness a sea of black hair on the heads of the audience, not a blond in the house – except Rod of course. The show went well but Rod, Pete and I had to rush out very quickly as we were to catch a flight back to London that night. I had to come home to apply for another working visa for the US and more importantly Bun was coming to stay with me at Waterford Road. I remained in touch with her as best I could while we were touring and couldn't wait to see her.

I met her at Heathrow and was really nervous about seeing her and how she would look after all that surgery on her face. In fact I was astonished at how well she looked although she was still in a bit of a state and understandably very emotional. We stayed in London for a couple of weeks as there was a bit of a wait until I got my new working visa, but then we were on our way back to LA where I was due to start to start working on Rod's next album *Tonight I'm Yours*.

6

CRUDELIS SED JUSTI

One day did two double takes
For standing there was Hattie Jacques,
Married her… good luck God bless
Creaking beds at Eardley Cres,
You did some plays with quite short runs
Hattie gave you two nice sons
(I don't know why I'm writing this
You'll read it and you'll take the piss).

Ode to John Le Mesurier by Clive Dunn

It was very difficult for Bun after the accident. You can't go through something like that without the experience taking its toll physically and psychologically. Bun was traumatised and, for a while, was very difficult. I'll leave this to her to explain, 'It was a nightmare after the car crash. I turned into a horrible, weird, scared, angry person. Robin dealt with it and I don't know how. The pain killing drugs took their toll. I'd say crazy shit to him and it would just like roll off. I used to say to him, it's not my fault, I can't control *her* – it wasn't like it was me – I was another person. It got better as time went on but the first year was hell for him and for me.' Reading this description is sort of disconcerting because to me it didn't seem as if she was behaving badly at all in the circumstances – but I knew she was suffering.

After about a month Bun went to work behind the scenes with the 'Bunny Mothers'. The Bunny Mothers were former employees, who inspected the working Bunnies before they started their shifts to ensure that they were displaying exactly the right 'Playboy Bunny Image'. In fact, the Playboy organisation was incredibly supportive and all her friends were great with Bun. She covered up the scars with makeup and didn't go back to work 'on the floor' for about six months after the accident.

Bun and I were now living in West Hollywood; about a ten minute walk to The Record Plant where we were recording *Tonight I'm Yours*. Harry Nilsson used to come around to the house quite regularly at that time. I can't recall how we met but he became a great friend. He used to call and say, 'I'm in the neighbourhood, can I come around?' And he did. And he stayed. Fortunately he was great company and our evenings were enhanced by the use of drugs. It was at this time that I was doing quite a lot of coke. To be honest, cocaine was something else and, for me, was a relatively new experience. I loved the instant high I got from it and the confidence it seemed to give me. I suppose I should say I had a love/hate relationship with the drug as I realised that I could easily have become addicted. But luckily I was one of those rare people who could say no after a few lines. Harry Nilson and I could stay up for hours on end and it was always such a pleasure having him over. It was a great loss when he died. One of my favourite albums is *A little Touch Of Schmilsson in the Night*. Recorded in one session, it was arranged by Nelson Riddle. A beautiful recording.

The group had actually started rehearsing on *Tonight I'm Yours* before I got back to LA because of the delay in obtaining my visa, which was a bit annoying, but Billy Gaff managed to sort it all out and I was delighted to be back 'home' and working. We spent a couple of months in the studio, and, next door at L'Entourage, a great restaurant run by four 'black foot' French Moroccan brothers. George, Albert, Robert and Michel. Of course, this was long before mobile phones and so we had a direct telephone line from the studio to the restaurant where all the members of the band could be contacted and any of us could go and do an overdub or a solo without wasting any time. I remember Kevin describing the scene as, 'Like spitfire pilots scrambling for their planes when the call went out that they were needed at the studio.'

The record Plant was founded owned and run by a wonderful man, Chris Stone, who sadly passed away in September 2016, aged eighty-one, following a heart attack and stroke. I attended a memorial service – a celebration of his life, where the inscription on cocktail napkins read, 'Even though the song has ended, the melody lingers on.' In 1970, the studio became one of the first to offer a 24-track recorder and believe it or not, installed a jacuzzi for use by the artists. Chris wanted the musicians to feel so much at home that he described the space as, 'the artists' living room.'

Chris was true to his word. He was always so accommodating and after he realised we were spending so much time next door at the restaurant, he built us our own 'pub' at the studio. I cannot imagine anyone else being so obliging. We called it The Dog and Clitoris. Say no more. As soon as the recording session was over, we would inevitably head for the pub. We installed a dartboard by the front door and came close to skewering visitors on a number of occasions. Probably not the most sensible – but then we didn't really do sensible. Jim Cregan owned a throwing knife about nine inches long which he used to practice throwing whenever he got a chance and one day, he was playing darts against soul singer and producer Bobby Womack. Bobby had thrown his three darts and Jim, instead of finishing his set with a dart, actually launched the knife into the bullseye, it went through the board and embedded itself deep in the door. Bobby actually turned white...

I'm reminded of the time we were there recording with Lion. There was a drinks dispenser halfway down the hall which sold 'Long Necked Budweiser Beers' for the very cheap price of twenty-five cents each. I wondered then if I could make a photocopy of a one dollar bill to acquire four of the beers. But... NO... it didn't work. So I tried copying a twenty dollar bill, and YES... it seemed to trick the dispenser perfectly. After a few weeks of getting free drinks, my guilt overcame me and I went to tell Chris about the fault in the machine. He just smiled at me and said something like, 'Clever bugger, aren't you? Don't worry about it.' Of course he fixed the problem straightaway.

While we were with Rod, we had what was called a 'lock out' so no one else could use our studio. We would arrive at noonish and spend much time sitting around in a circle throwing musical ingredients into the mix as it were to see what came up. There was always much silliness going on in the band. One day I unscrewed the top of Rod's microphone and inserted a piece of raw fish into it. Hours went by while he was sniffing his clothing and everything around him, trying to figure where the stench was coming from. Everyone else knew what and where the offending odour came from, and it was very difficult to restrain the guffaws of laughter. Eventually I had to tell Rod, and graciously he had to admit that was a great ruse.

Halfway through the recording of *Tonight I'm Yours*, it was decided that we should change the personnel of group and Carmine Appice was sacked. A couple of us, and I was the most vociferous, suggested we bring in Tony Brock. Tony was in the original Stryder and we worked together in Limey before he joined The Babys. Carmine was understandably most upset about the change.

In his autobiography, *Stick It!*, he wrote that he wasn't being given a production credit, for which he blamed Jim and so 'slammed Cregan up against a studio wall and told him... I'd kick his ass'. Jim doesn't remember this, but does recall throwing his guitar at Carmen Appice.

A few words about Carmine. He was Vanilla Fudge's drummer and was in the eponymous Beck, Bogart and Appice. To call him a larger than life character is a bit of an understatement. He liked to describe himself as a legend and wasn't exactly modest about his ability or his womanising. He was a bit more of a shrinking violet when it came to sharing outgoings. It's always important for band members to pay your way – you'd soon get ostracised if you didn't. We would take it in turns to pay for meals and it was just pure chance on the amount you might have to cough up. It could cost you about $150 if you were lucky or the bill might amount to $1000, depending on the circumstances. But Carmine was the type of guy who would either make himself scarce when the bill came or announce, 'I only had a salad', throw in a ten dollar bill and then quickly disappear. After a while we decided that we had had enough; I think it was in Munich that the band were having lunch and each one of us made an excuse to leave the table – pretending to go to the toilet or whatever. He was left with the bill and actually ended up in tears. He was also well known for taking food from breakfast trays outside our rooms when we had finished eating. Carmine had brought Danny and Jay into the band and later on, I discovered that he had told them that if they were to get any songs on the next record, he wanted a percentage. Bloody cheek. Even after he was sacked and replaced by Tony Brock who was brilliant, he asked if he could tour with the band and do Tony's drum solos. Unbelievable!

When Carmine went we also said goodbye to Marvin. Carmine's wife Marlene had this glove puppet – a lion called Marvin, which she used to bring out and do a sort of ventriloquist act. It was amusing at first, but then became very annoying and even Carmine found it embarrassing. Anyway, we had had enough of Marvin after a while and kidnapped him.

This was instigated by Billy Francis, who was our security guy for many years during those days. He handled all the practical matters and was what we used to describe as 'a rough diamond'. He always had a great sense of humour. I don't think we sent Marlene a ransom note but when she realised that Marvin had disappeared, she went bonkers – it was if her child had been kidnapped. After about a month, during which Marlene was distraught and had driven us even more mad, and following an entreaty by Carmine, Jim Cregan decided enough was enough and engineered Marvin's return.

We were at the Rainbow having dinner and a few drinks. Marlene ordered a Caesar salad and somehow, it just happened that Marvin was served up with the salad. Marlene was utterly overjoyed when she and Marvin were re-united. We weren't…

When we shot the cover for *Tonight I'm Yours*, which was released in November 1981, Carmine was in the photo shoot but later for the reprint of the cover Tony was in the photograph. We all got a little drunk and very jolly during the shoot, so we thought it would be a good idea to go on to The Rainbow for some more drinks. 'Boiler' was dressed in an English bobby's uniform, directing traffic on Sunset Boulevard. The real cops arrived and were dissuaded from arresting us after much pleading of innocence and trying the old, 'Do you know who we are?' line. I think Rod was the only one who could pull that off.

It was decided that 'Young Turks' and the title track, 'Tonight I'm Yours' would be the first two singles from the album. So videos had to be made. MTV was very much a music video channel in those days – such a pity it has changed so much now. Anyway, 'Young Turks' was shot in downtown LA by some train tracks and this was all fairly uneventful, but 'Tonight I'm Yours' was a completely different kettle of fish. We had taken over the entire courtyard of The Sunset Marquis, a very famous rock 'n' roll hotel and known for its celebrity clientele in the heart of West Hollywood. The hotel had a pool, which many of the rooms faced. It was a late evening/night shoot with an enormous amount of booze and scantily clad girls around the pool and in every room. For good measure there was even a small boat in the pool with a couple of girls rowing around. At one point Jim Cregan got thrown into the pool with his beloved 'Zematis' guitar. Luckily the instrument didn't suffer any damage. But close to the end of the shoot, Alana turned up and put a stop to the whole thing. There was more than enough footage for the edit. I'm sure it's available to view on 'YouTube'.

On a more sombre memory, it was during the week of making that video, Russ Shaw, who was our sometime publicist, died of AIDS. He was the first person I knew who contracted and lost his life to that awful disease. It was the early 80s and the beginning of a terrible worldwide epidemic.

God, I've lost so many friends in the last few years.

I became involved in a few other projects before touring with Rod. Stuart Taylor was a record producer I had known for a few years and he asked me to write and record an instrumental single entitled 'The Axeman Cometh'. So I just had to write, with tongue firmly in cheek, a piece of 'heavy metal music'. We recorded it in LA with the help of the guys from Lion. I took the master reel back to London and had the London Symphony Orchestra play to the track. It turned out very well I thought, but not one single label wanted to release it. I suppose nothing like that had ever been done before and they all thought it was too risky. Funnily enough, not long after that I worked on an album of orchestrated Police songs called *Arrested* with The Royal Philharmonic Orchestra and various artists that did quite well. Go figure…

Working with Ronnie Wood is always a laugh. I'd been in the studio, inevitably The Record Plant with him, recording his solo album, *1-2-3-4*, which was released in September 1981 and featured Ian McLagan, Bobby Womack, Charlie Watts and Bobby Keys among others. To be honest, most of the time was spent fooling around and making each other laugh. One day it was decided that we should all wear hats. The more ridiculous… the better. At the time, the only thing I had was a tartan 'cheese cutter', a sort of flat cap. I can't remember who wore what except Ronnie turned up in an enormous cowboy hat that was about three feet in width.

Not long after I did the album with 'Woody', the sound engineer Ricky Delena and I went to visit him at a house he was renting on Mandeville Canyon, close to The Pacific Palisades just off Sunset Boulevard. Ian McLagan and Charlie Watts were there as well. I think they were supposed to be rehearsing for something or other. Anyway, Charlie was keeping himself to himself as he does, and the rest of us were having a drink and just being generally silly. At one point in the evening, Ronnie said, 'Mac and I are just going out for a bit, we'll be back soon.' Ricky and I said, 'Fine see you in a while.'

Well, 'a bit' became an a hour and then two hours and then three at which point I decided I didn't want to hang around any longer and had no idea when they would be back. Apparently, they returned a couple of days later… but without the car and no idea where their automobile was. I can only imagine what they got up to. I can't say for sure as I never bothered to find out. It was par for the course.

Before we were to start the Tonight I'm Yours tour, (aka Le Grand tour) we went to New York to do a television recording on NBC called *Saturday Night Live,* which is now a very famous, long running satirical comedy series. It was the cult show that really kick started the careers of the likes of John Belushi, Steve Martin, Dan Ackroyd and Eddie Murphy. We were to perform 'Tonight I'm Yours' and 'Hot Legs'. Gary Grainger was supposed to fly over from England for the show. He got on the plane at Heathrow but at the last minute got off the plane and refused to re-board. The same problem he had encountered when we were doing the American Music Awards show. Somehow, Pete Buckland managed to persuade him to summon up his courage and actually got him on Concord to make the show.

Not long after, Gary decided not to join us for the upcoming tour so we needed a third guitarist for the duration. Our immediate thought was Wally Stocker, who was also in The Babys with Tony Brock, and a fine guitar player. Pete Buckland, Jim Cregan and I went to see Rod at his beach house, just a little up the coast in Trancas. The house looked like a miniature version of The Sidney Opera House. I'm not sure which building went up first. Anyway, we told Rod about Gary's decision, to which he stated, 'Tour's off!' Then we told him that we had Wally 'Tour's on!' was his response. It was that simple!

When I joined Rod's band I was bombarded with sponsorship and endorsement deals from guitar makers (Aria, Kramer, Fernandes) and amplifier firms, (Hiwatt and Peavey) as well as string manufacturers. It seems to me a bit of a dichotomy that those of us who could afford to buy them were given the equipment. There was no contract – just the permission to use quotes and photographs for publicity, whereas upcoming groups had to go and buy all the gear they needed. But I do understand the logic behind the endorsements.

When I first started to play the guitar, I would practice every waking minute and consequently the strings used to wear out frequently. So I heard of a trick which involved taking the old strings off and boiling them to clean the dirt and sweat off them. Now, you could do this a few times but eventually you just had to give in and buy a new set. And another thing: in those days in the early sixties, there wasn't a great deal of choice when buying strings. You couldn't find 'light gauge strings', i.e. it was very hard to bend strings to a certain note. So I heard that Eric Clapton used to buy banjo strings because they were thinner. Now banjo strings don't have a 'ball' on the end of them so I had to keep the 'balls' (pardon the expression) from the ones I had discarded and wrap the banjo string around the 'ball'. Time consuming but it worked a treat. Now I could bend the strings with ease. And while I'm on the subject, let me introduce you to my guitars: 'Norman' and 'Ernest' (Strats) and 'Ronnie' and 'Keith' (James Trussart) and 'Robin' (Gibson Acoustic Dove), named by a tech. These are the guitars I usually take on tour with me. I don't use pedals or any type of other equipment to create a different effect.

One time I was doing a photo shoot with Eddie Van Halen, as we both endorsed Kramer Guitars. We knew each other so I thought it would be a fun thing to do. We met at a studio in Hollywood sometime in the afternoon and sat around and chatted for a while until we were to start the session. The photographer asked us if we would like a drink, Eddie and I looked at each other with wide grins and said, 'Why not?' We were handed a bottle of Jose Cuervo Gold tequila and finished it off in a very short space of time. Needless to say we were both drunk by the end of the session. I went into the dressing room and slipped and fell.

Meet Norman, Ernest, Ronnie and some of my other mates.

The bridge of my nose hit the edge of the table and that was that, I was out cold with concussion. I don't even remember being driven home. To this day I will never drink that variety of tequila, but almost any other is fine with me. Every time I see a bottle of Jose Cuervo Gold it reminds me of that shoot and the disastrous consequences.

In mid December 1981 I decided to fly my dad and Joannie out to the States to see us in San Francisco and at The 'Fabulous' Forum, one of the main arenas in LA. It was a great feeling to be able to treat them to a holiday as it were. Bun met them at LAX and I had arranged First Class tickets for the three of them to catch the 'Talgo' train to San Francisco – a beautiful journey up the Pacific coast. There was a bar on the train, with a piano and I believe Dad played it most of the way there!

We were staying at The Fairmont – an extremely luxurious hotel atop Nob Hill. At this time Jim Cregan was having an affair with Princess Diana Al Fassi. One of Sheik Al Fassi's many wives. It was all kept under the rug but she still needed to have security with her everywhere. She flew in a private Boeing 727 and had booked the entire penthouse of the hotel, which I think was deemed 'The Presidential Suite'. We were merciless with Jim and teased him about his new found luxurious lifestyle. We made requests for our own private helicopters, 'Actually, Jim, you know I ordered a green one, well, I've changed my mind. I want a yellow one. Can you sort that out for me?' The suite was enormous, having its own two storey library and observatory and a dining room which could seat twenty-eight people, over which a butler, in tailcoat, presided. There was also a huge lounge with a piano. Dad entertained us all until the early hours with Noel Coward standards like 'London Pride' and 'A Room With a View' and we had a wonderful sing-song until it all got a little too noisy and we were asked to leave. Fair enough, but a fabulous evening was had by all.

The following night Dad and Joannie came to the show. But beforehand they came backstage to the hospitality room where there was inevitably a lively, party atmosphere. I remember Dad remarking how different it was from the mood of an actor's dressing room before a performance, where he needed some peace and quiet. They were taken to their seats in the VIP section – and even in those days security was tight.

Joannie described the concert in her book, 'The show was great –

Robin cool and relaxed. Rod leapt about like a teenager and the crowd was happily hysterical, but half way through the second set a barrier broke and the audience surged forward. We were stranded and had no way of making it backstage when suddenly a team of bodyguards appeared, we were lifted aloft and passed over the heads of the crowd to the back of the stage where a fleet of limousines was waiting. The musicians appeared and pouring with sweat leapt into the safety of the cars and back to the sanctuary of the hotel. On the way the driver was playing pop music but Robin asked him to switch it off. He could not bear to hear any music during these tours, just occasionally something classical and serene. John was very proud of Robin and what he had achieved entirely through his own efforts.'

We then played four shows at the Forum where we were escorted on to the stage by a massed band of Scottish pipers in kilts and all the trimmings. One show was transmitted live to the UK in cinemas, and live on television in the USA. Jake went to see it in Leicester Square and he told me that the show was blacked out when the commercials were being broadcast in the States so some of the show was missed. It was a stupid mistake on management's behalf. Tina Turner and Bonnie Tyler, (or Tiny Boiler as we called her) came and joined us on a couple of songs on that show. I think we did one of Bonnie's hits at the time and Tina did 'Get Back' and 'Hot Legs' and the crowd adored her. She was lovely with us and totally down to earth – unlike some divas I could name... but won't.

I arranged 'All Access' passes for Steve Webb when I played at the Forum and we met at the backstage bar. Steve asked me how I was doing and I replied, 'A bit nervous.' Someone had telephoned the venue, threatening to shoot Rod and during the quiet part of 'Sailing', some idiot let off a fire cracker. It made us all jump, although luckily we didn't dive for cover. We all got a bit of a shock though.

After every concert we would leave immediately afterwards to avoid traffic. At those shows, we hired a London double decker bus to take us to the venue and back to the hotel. And if we had guests, the cardinal rule was that they had to be ready to leave when the group left the stage. Unfortunately the night that Joannie and Dad came with Bun, they were not where they were meant to be and I couldn't find Dad or Joannie – so we had to leave without them. It turned out they were in

Sailing with (from left) Me, Bun, Jim Cregan, Kelly Emberg and 'The Singer'.

The Forum Bar. And it took them ages before they made it back to the hotel.

After we had finished our Forum commitments, Rod threw a lavish Christmas party at his house on Carolwood Drive to which Dad and Joannie came. It was a great bash and Joannie recorded her memories in *Lady Don't Fall Backwards*, 'The drive was lined with flunkies in knee breeches holding flaming torches to greet us on arrival. The house was enormous and the whole place twinkled with stars. To my delight I spotted Gregory Peck and Farrah Fawcett with Ryan O'Neal. There was a Pre-Raphaelite room, a Tiffany room and a ballroom in the centre of which was a Christmas tree, which reached to the roof. At the far end was a minstrel's gallery housing a jazz group to which John gravitated immediately.'

I extricated Dad from the jazz musicians and introduced him to Gregory Peck. He told the great Hollywood star, 'I'm a great fan of yours.' To which Gregory replied, 'And I'm such a fan of yours.' Dad was astonished and delighted – in his own quiet inimitable way – and they chatted away for some time. Dad had a wonderful time at the party and I recall him approaching Rod at one stage in the evening in the aptly named 'powder room' just near the bar and asking, 'You don't by chance have anything here for my left nostril?' Rod replied, 'Yes, of course, John, come with me.' The three of us snuck into a small bathroom and well… I don't think I have to explain any more – other than to add that I think Dad found something for his right nostril as well.

Rod's family was also at the party, having come over to spend Christmas with him. Rod's mum remarked to Dad, 'Our boys have done us proud, John.' It was so good to have Dad and Joannie there for a couple of weeks. It was wonderful having Dad there on my turf, so to speak I think it was the last time I spent that amount of time with dad for that long. Dad actually talked about the guilt at not being around when Jake and I were young and we were able to bond properly for the first time in years.

The tour started again in the New Year and went very well until we arrived in Boston in February. Not a good idea to arrive in Boston in the winter – particularly in a blizzard that lasted five days. We were snowbound for five days as ten foot drifts enveloped the hotel. We only had the clothes we stood up in as our bags had already gone ahead in trucks on their way to Providence, Rhode Island, where our next concert was supposed to take place. We were staying at a very stuffy but nice hotel and we weren't allowed into the bar or restaurant without a jacket or tie. So we found a thrift shop and bought the most tasteless clothes we could find; a selection of kipper ties, Hawaiian shirts and garish jackets so we could be accepted in the restaurant while still cocking a snook at the rules.

We contacted Billy Gaff to say that we were stuck and asked what he was going to do about it to which he tearfully replied, 'Do what you want. I've been fired.' So we were stuck in Boston without any management to sort things out and not knowing what to do. Rod decreed he would never ever do a tour of North America in winter and from then on we would always go south for winter tours.

I called the office in LA and asked for the money owed to them to be wired to Boston (band members were receiving a percentage of the takings – not on a salary).The money was being handled by Gayle Williams and I asked her for $5,000 but was told by Gayle that there was no money. We had been on the road for months and so the band was pretty upset. I told Rod and we later discovered that Billy Gaff had been siphoning money from the account for some time. The money was found from somewhere else and we were paid. So Rod fired Billy Gaff and never worked with him again. Poor old Pete Buckland, caught in the crossfire, left the organisation, although he was absolutely blameless. There was a subsequent court case in which a settlement was negotiated although Billy Gaff was in violation of Californian law by acting as manager, record label and music publisher simultaneously.

In any case, the band recorded and toured worldwide and I soon found myself in a sort of *Spinal Tap* travelling circus. We were flying around the world in private jets, riding in luxury limos, consuming cocaine in huge quantities and encircled by groupies at every gig. During the various tours with the Rod Stewart, I have to admit there was much debauchery and foolish behaviour. The chemistry in the band was really good and it was like enjoying a working holiday with your best mates most of the time. Rod's philosophy for the band was that we should have fun. We should always be ultra professional on stage but enjoying ourselves was paramount. Nothing was ever taken too seriously and rehearsals were always punctuated by beers and cocktails. Being on the road was pretty boring much of the time and so we used to alleviate the tedium by playing practical jokes and so the band and crew invented a sort of gang of alter egos, who we called 'The Sex Police'.

Rod described it pretty well, 'Our founding intention was to stamp out sex on the road – to identify, within the touring party, the likely practitioners of sex, locate the places in which sex might take place and prevent sex from happening… even the Sex Police feared a knock on the door from the Sex Police.' As time went by our 'missions' became more varied and imaginative.

We wore white boiler suits when we went to work, carried tool kits and screwdrivers for more complex operations, hid walkie-talkies about our bodies, secreted cameras for evidence purposes and indulged in the use of ropes and handcuffs whenever necessary. We all had nicknames – Patrick Logue (Boiler) because he had a big unsightly boil on the back of his neck. I was 'Major Bucks' and Pete Buckland was 'Gruppenführer' (group leader) until later, when I took over from him, and Jim Cregan, because he liked sailing, was given the name of 'Seaman Stains'. Other members were 'Corporal Punishment', 'Major Disruption' and 'Private Parts'.

This was an organisation to be feared by all – but particularly if you were American. Band members were chained to beds, the contents of hotel rooms were emptied into lifts and bedroom doors were removed. Most of the band were married or with partners – although, that didn't make any difference to the inclinations of the musicians. In a hotel in Chicago we heard that there were two girls in Jay Davis' room. I managed to get a pass key and we burst into his bedroom – Jay was in bed fully clothed as were the two young women either side of him. There was absolutely nothing going on, but we still took a photograph with Jay's camera. He completely forgot about it and later on when the film was developed, his wife discovered the print. She wasn't best pleased but he placated her by buying her a new set of boobs.

Part of our entourage was Louise Fisher, who started doing hair and make-up for Rod, but became the group's mum and 'nurse'. When we got bored, we would draw pictures of our own knobs and then pass the sketches to Louise to see if she could recognise them – now this wasn't because Louise was a groupie – but she seemed to know exactly whose was whose. In my case it was because whenever she knocked at the door, I'd give myself some time, call for her to come in and made sure I had stripped naked. I don't know how she recognised the other members of the band's members… if you see what I mean. The band would give their passports to Pete Buckland, but then Rod would demand them and draw all sorts of rude pictures in the passports. Rod once designed a visa from East Cheam in mine.

In Germany we had a new bass player, Brit Charlie Harrison, who had been in the Californian band country rock band Poco. We managed to get a key to Rod's suite, kidnapped Charlie and gaffer taped him to Rod's bed. When Rod returned to his room, he was completely unconcerned, simply said, 'Hello Charlie,' left him there and arranged to be moved to another suite. The keyboard player John Corey was the only single guy in the group – a lovely bloke but always on the pull. We once stuffed all his clothes in a suitcase and lowered it four floors. We took the hinge off his door so when he put the key in his lock the door just fell off and crashed to the floor. We emptied the room of as much furniture as we could fit into the lift.

Changes of costume for Rod – or breaks – used to take place in a space under the stage and one of Boiler's favourite pranks was to regularly strip off for no apparent reason. He would be naked apart from his socks and whenever we would discover him in this state, and utter something like, 'Oh Boiler… not again?' he would just shrug his exposed shoulders and reply, 'What? What's the problem?' Boiler would put peanuts in Jimmy Zavala's harmonica and talc in his saxophone. It was most amusing for us and most annoying for Jimmy. He also wrote instructions on the stage where Jimmy would stand such as, 'No dancing', 'Behave yourself', etc. etc.

At one point, in the mid-west during an American tour, Rod was doing an interview with the legendary presenter of *American Bandstand*, Dick Clark, an American institution in broadcasting, and for some reason we decided to buy a dozen live chickens to be released into the hotel suite during the taping. The timing was perfect; just as the interview was being wrapped up, someone shouted, 'room service' and we burst in, releasing the chickens from their boxes. Mayhem ensued; feathers and chicken shit were everywhere. Dick Clark freaked out and jumped on the sofa. The whole thing was on tape too.

We were lucky in the fact that we always had the use of a private plane on the tours. We used two private Lear jets (Four Engine Viscount Turbo props) to get around – no buses for us! We nicknamed one of them The Flying Ashtray – for the smokers amongst us. We made another TV appearance during that time. My friend, Larry Greene, a CBS cameraman worked on the show *Entertainment Tonight*. I convinced him to do a segment on the band, which we recorded in Oklahoma. As we landed, instead of three limousines, we were met by nine yellow cabs to take us to the hotel. It was quite a sight. Poor Larry was killed in 2002, while on special assignment in the Persian Gulf. The US Navy helicopter, in which he was riding, crashed into a Syrian freighter. Four navy personnel survived.

In 1983, we recorded a single, 'Infatuation', for the *Camouflage* album. Jeff Beck played a solo on the number and it made the charts. Jeff joined us for a tour the following year. The trouble was he only played on a few songs including 'Infatuation' and he didn't really like this 'supporting' role. We didn't think he would stick it out for very long – in fact we had a betting syndicate between us about how long he would last. I think he stayed with the band for five shows and wasn't happy. He wasn't at all big time – in fact he's very self deprecating. I'm very fond of him and I think he's one of the best guitarists around – I'm pleased to say that the respect is mutual. After one of the Earl's Court gigs, Jeff and I went to Tramp and he told me, 'You're fucking dangerous!' I take it that Jeff was referring to my guitar playing and not my character.

The same year, we were in Cannes shooting another single, 'What am I going to do' ('I'm so in love with you?') We rented a schooner, a 1920's clipper called 'Shenandoah', and owned by the King of Denmark. There was a fully stocked bar on board which wasn't a good idea – or maybe it was. There were a lot of high jinks, in which a bass guitar went overboard. Afterwards, we had a camp fire on the beach and we were miming to the track. There were a number of babes – model types and dancers still hanging around. As it was getting dark, Alana arrived and pulled Rod away. Not for the first or last time. And that... was the end of the shoot.

At the beginning of June I came to England for a football match. Not just any old game, but an England v Scotland game at Wembley. Those of you who know me understand that I am not a football fan but

Do you think we're sexy? Me, Kevin Savigar, Bernie Boyle and Rod (ANNIE CHALLIS)

Rod got tickets for me and Jim Cregan and we thought it would be fun. We stayed in the Dorchester and while I was in England, I decided to treat myself to a 'Full English' breakfast. I rang room service and made my request and about five minutes later there was a knock on my door and there was my breakfast order. I was amazed that the service was so quick – only to be told that this very classy hotel had a kitchen on every floor and so as to provide an incredibly quick response to any room service requests. A bit different to my early days of 'beans or tomatoes!'

Anyway the international was the same day as the Derby and so I rang my dad and asked who I should bet on. His reply was unambiguous, 'Lester Piggott of course.' Before the match we went around to Rod's parents' house in Archway Road and I walked around to the bookie's where I placed two £5 bets on England and Lester Piggott winning. They both came in – Lester on Teenoso at 9-2 and England beating Scotland 2-0 – and I was literally 'quids in'.

It was a great day out at Wembley. Rod's dad and his two brothers Donnie and Rob were with us as well as a few other people. Rod hired a small coach for the outing and drinks inevitably flowed there and back. Later that evening Rod, Jim and I went out on the town to a restaurant and then on to Tramp. On the way in the car we played 'spot the jock', a silly game like 'I spy', pointing out all the Scots we could see on the streets. Rod was devastated that Scotland lost, which was just as enjoyable...

There was one gig that same month that was particularly memorable, as described in the preface. The concert at Earl's Court on 25th June 1983. At the time, we had a number one hit with 'Baby Jane' and we were on tour in Europe which included three shows at Earl's Court Exhibition Centre. There had been a hiccup on the first night. We were staying The Holiday Inn in Swiss Cottage, but the bus driving to the venue was stuck in traffic on Park Lane for what seemed like an eternity. We were getting very late and time was running out. I didn't want to be late for this special show and, knowing the area very well, I suggested we take public transport. So, we got off the bus at St James's Park underground station, boarded a tube train and made our way to the venue. When we arrived at the entrance to Exhibition Centre, we explained to the security guy why we were on foot and a bit late. He looked at us with disbelief and said, 'You're the Rod Stewart Group?

Pull the other one! Bugger off, you're not coming in here.' Luckily we found one of our crew and, very begrudgingly, he let us through the front doors. A typical 'jobsworth'.

Joannie had gone on holiday to Spain and Marion, a cousin of hers, had moved into the Ramsgate house to look after Dad and the cats because, as Joannie described, 'none of whom had mastered the knack of opening a can of food.' Dad and Marion came to see me after the show with Joan Sims and we all enjoyed a few drinks together. Dad hired a car to take them back to Ramsgate and according to Marion, Dad cried a lot on the way home and was 'tired and melancholy the following day.' Not like him at all.

I received a letter from Dad a day after the last concert.

28 June 1983

Dearest Robin,
Thankyou for all the pleasure you gave to so many people last Saturday evening including Marion and Joan Sims and Me. I only wish Joan had been there. She would have been proud of you. It was also good to see and Talk with Kim. A Rare Happening. As always PA xx
PS Please Write sometime.

It wasn't long after this that Dad became ill. At home in Ramsgate, he suffered a haemorrhage and he was immediately admitted to the local hospital. I was still touring with Rod in Europe and happened to have an impacted wisdom tooth. Although I had to get back on tour as soon as possible, I came back to England to have surgery and I went down to Kent to see him for a couple of days.

I was quite nervous about the visit as Joannie told me he was really not well. When I got to the hospital it was indeed a shock. He looked so frail and gaunt that it took my breath away. But, of course, he put on quite a good show for me desperately trying to be humorous to make me feel better, but I could see he was not long for this earth. That was pretty hard to see him so unwell. But at least I was there and got to see him. The next day I was off again to return to the Rod tour we were doing in Europe.

Dad came home after a week, but by then I was back on tour. We kept in touch by telephone as much as I could. Jake was living back at Waterford Road and visited Dad as often as he could manage. Sadly the following month Dad became unwell, his condition gradually deteriorated and he became critically ill.

A few days before he died, Dad said to Joan, 'Darling I'm fed up of it now and I think I'd like to die.' Joan wrote about it in her book, *Dear John*, 'He held my hand tightly and said, "It's all been rather lovely." Being 'fed up of it' came from one of Clive (Corporal Jones in *Dad's Army*) and Cilla Dunn's children, close family friends for many years. Apparently their daughter became bored during a matinee at the theatre and in the middle of a dramatic silence, said very loudly, "I'm fed up of it now and I want to go home."'

Dad never regained consciousness. He died of cirrhosis of the liver and the following announcement appeared in the obituary column of *The Times:* 'John Le Mesurier wishes it be known that he 'conked out' on 15th November. He sadly misses family and friends.'

I had been applying for a green card (permanent residency in the US) and when Mum died, I had managed to obtain a letter of parole (a document which allows one to leave the US and return without a visa) from the US Government which enabled me to return for the funeral, but when Dad passed away I was refused a similar letter from The Immigration and Naturalization Service so I couldn't enter the UK for fear of not being allowed back in the US. They wouldn't even let me attend my own father's funeral! I consequently had to drop my petition to get my green card and start the whole application again – which took me another year. I think all the difficulties in the process may have had something to do with John Lennon whose own application was complicated by a drugs conviction.

The private funeral in Ramsgate was followed by a memorial service a few months later at the Actors' Church St Paul's, Covent Garden. Fortunately, Bun and I did get to go to this commemoration of Dad's life. On the front door to the church, a deflated inner tube was hung there as an homage to Jacques Tati's classic film *Monsieur Hulot's Holiday*. I think you have to have seen the movie to understand the connection. Jacques Tati was my dad's idol and he had introduced me to the great Frenchman's work years previously. In fact to this day whenever I watch

Dad with my wicked stepmother, Joannie (JON LYONS/REX/SHUTTERSTOCK)

a Tati movie it always reminds me of Dad. My favourite is *Jour de Fete*, a real classic.

At the service, the score to *Monsieur Hulot's Holiday* was played and Bill Pertwee (the warden in *Dad's Army*) made us all laugh with a wonderfully witty tribute. This was followed by a recording of Dad reciting an Indian poem which he had always loved.

When I am dead, cry for me a little,
When I am dead, think of me sometimes,
But not too much, think of me as I was in life at some moment,
if it is pleasant to recall, But not too much.
Leave me in peace, and I shall leave you in my peace,
And while you live, let your thoughts be with the living.

The tribute ended with Annie Ross singing 'What's New?' – one of Dad's and Joan's favourite numbers. The party continued until the wee hours – Bruce Copp inevitably concocted a lovely buffet meal, the stories and anecdotes about Dad flowed, as did the laughter, wine and dope. It was indeed a wonderful celebration of his life.

Soon after Dad's death at the end of November 1983, while still awaiting provision of a green card Bun and I decided to return to England and so we moved to the Waterford Road house that had been left to Jake and I (I later bought Jake's share in the house from him). We ended up staying there about four years and I was able to travel to and from the US on work visas, which seemed pretty weird at the time, as they didn't want me as a permanent resident.

It was a lovely house and very central, but we hadn't been there long when we were besieged by the paparazzi. Rod had stayed there as had Julian Lennon, who was a good friend and the press saw Waterford Rd as being a rock star hangout – some sort of rock 'n' roll safe house. It was true that at most times we were there, you could have created quite a supergroup.

At that time, there had been a report in one of the tabloids that one of Madonna's staff had punched a photographer. One evening, Bun and I were getting ready to go to the cinema when there was a knock at the door. It was a journalist, who had been hiding outside the house. He was convinced that Bun was Madonna and I was the guy that had thumped the photographer. Not only case of mistaken identity, but also of character. I could never have been a contender. I was often being mistaken for other people. Once in a restaurant in Soho, a woman insisted that I was one of the Rolling Stones and no matter how many times I denied it, she was absolutely convinced I was 'a Stone'. Eventually I gave up protesting and when she demanded my autograph, I caved in and signed it, 'Brian Jones'.

Another visitor to the house was film and television star Robert Wagner. We met him through his step daughter, Katie, who is a reporter and journalist, and who lived with us for a while when she came to London to do some modelling. Robert who is known to family and friends as 'RJ' visited us in London regularly and we often had dinner together. I recall one Indian meal when we were joined by Bryan Forbes and Nanette Newman. Bryan just wanted to talk about Dad all evening – the interest in him and Mum from friends was something I had happily grown used to over the years.

One of my favourite stories concerning Forbes and Newman concerned our old family friend, Peter Sellers. At a dinner party, Peter suddenly announced to Bryan Forbes that he was going to marry Nanette Newman. Bryan politely pointed out that he was actually still married to Nanette Newman and planned to remain so. Sellers seemed unimpressed and no doubt pressed on with his marital plans. What I don't know is how Nanette Newman responded to this conversation! With good grace, I imagine, knowing Peter's reputation.

When I returned to live in LA I would sometimes stay at RJ's ranch style house, just off Mandeville Canyon. He loves horses and has stables. I'll never forget the wonderment of seeing a foal being born. RJ is a lovely guy and has treated me like a surrogate son, always greeting me with a cheery, 'Hello mate!' He and his sweet and glamorous wife, actress Jill St John, remain good friends to this day.

Another wonderful friend who I met during this time is Sherry Daly, who manages Charlie Watts and Ronnie Wood and is the director of production company Munro Sounds. I met Sherry during the period when I was living on and off at Waterford Road. The first time Sherry and her husband Steve came over for dinner, Sherry noticed all the photos of mum I had around the house and she said to me, 'You must be a big Hattie Jaques fan.' I said, 'I am. Probably the greatest. She's my mum…'

Sherry's entry into the rock 'n' roll world is amusingly circuitous. In the 1960s she worked for Prince Michael of Kent, who happened to be President of the *British Bobsleigh,* later to become the British Bobsleigh Association and who had actually competed for Great Britain in the 1971 World Bobsleigh Championships. Sherry met a couple of the guys in the Rolling Stones office who were into the sport and asked her to work in their office. One of the original Rolling Stones members, keyboard player Ian Stewart, forever known as 'the 6th Stone' who later worked as a road manager, asked Sherry to work full time in the office. Thirty-seven years later – she's still there!

Sherry used to live near Dad and Joan in Barons Court and would often see Dad, always dressed immaculately, making phone calls from a nearby telephone box. She couldn't understand why he would be doing this as she thought he must have had a telephone at home. I wouldn't be surprised if he was putting on a bet – unknown to Joannie! I sent Sherry a copy of *The Velveteen Rabbit*, which she loved and she said listening to Dad's voice always reminds her of me.

Gina Vaisey, originally a friend of Bun's, visited us in 1985, soon after we had moved in and we were doing up the house. She burned a hole in our new carpet with a cigarette before I had even met her. She was so ashamed and embarrassed; she covered the damage with a trivial pursuit board game which we played incessantly. There were questions about Mum and Dad in the game, which was weird.

With Rod's band, we played a huge event in January 1985. For an estimated crowd of nearly 300,000 people, in fact. This was quite something – and a first – for me to be playing to such a large audience. It was at the inaugural 'Rock in Rio' festival, which continued for ten days and for which the band were booked to headline twice – on the second day and about a week later. Also on the bill were Ozzy Osbourne, Queen, Yes, and The Go-Go's among others. Despite our fears that it would be typically South American and a bit chaotic, the festival was actually very well organised and there were giant banners on the famous waterfront greeting all the bands.

We stayed at the Copacabana Beach hotel and it just so happened that many of the musicians were also guests there. As we had a week to hang out between appearances, there was plenty of time for carousing. The partying went on most nights and every morning at the pool the walking wounded gathered in various states of recovery. One night we took all the Go-Go's on a dinner date. The Go-Go's were pretty wild – originally a punk band from LA, they were the first only all-female band to write their own material and play their own instruments to feature in the charts.

We booked Maxim's, the same company that has the famous Maxim's in Paris, and is actually infamous for being the Gestapo's headquarters during World War II. Unlike its French counterpart the food was terrible and even the waiter advised us to avoid the lamb, as 'the refrigeration here isn't safe!' So instead of tucking in to great grub, we just snacked on some appetizers and inevitably drank to excess. And that was just the start. Rod wrote in his autobiography 'after our second performance, back at the hotel, we took on the Go-Go's, Belinda Carlisle's all-girl rock group, in a coke snorting competition. This was a tactical error which someone, surely, should have been in a position to warn us about. Those girls could snort lacquer off a table. We lost heavily.' I couldn't possibly comment.

The festival was a great success and it's still going to this day though I believe it's now 'Rock in Rio US' and held in Las Vegas. Another extraordinary performance that is etched in my memory was at Jones Beach in New York State. That was quite a gig. The stage backed onto the Atlantic. There was a hurricane and when we came on stage it was torrential rain. The crowd were absolutely soaked but stuck with us. Unfortunately the canopy under which we were playing collapsed under the weight of the water and we were left open to the elements. One by one, each mic or instrument went out until only Rod's radio mic and the bass drum were working. Rod carried on like the trouper he is but 'Maggie May' didn't sound quite the same under those conditions, accompanied only by a bass drum.

A couple of years later, we were back touring in Europe. We were in Italy to play various places. I believe it was in Viareggio that they didn't have a suite for 'the singer', which is what we called Rod (and also how I refer to Johnny Hallyday). So, the hotel decided to knock a connecting wall between two rooms especially for him. In the end, we didn't stay there. But at least they have a suite now!

When in Milan, the plane was delayed on the morning we were supposed to leave. We were still in the hotel and so, of course, I went to the bar on the ground floor near the lobby. A local guy came into the bar and asked for an espresso and a Sambuca, an aniseed flavoured liqueur. He poured it into his coffee and downed it in one. 'That looks like something I should try,' I thought. I ordered one and did the same. It was an eye opener and tasted delicious! I immediately called Jim and Kevin to get down to the bar as quickly as they could. They were there in a few minutes and we all had one, two three, four. After four I lost count as and had so many because we wouldn't be leaving for another two hours or so. It's like a legal drug and we were hammered by the time we left. We had many more on that tour and the liqueur still sometimes takes my fancy these days.

On that same tour in 1986 we were also playing at the Bull Ring in Barcelona. There were literally a load of bulls penned behind the stage. It was very hot and smelly and also very loud – they must have been deafened by the music and could have caused a stampede. But that, it turned out, was the least of my worries.

We completed the sound check and went back to the hotel where I met up with Joannie and Bruce Copp, who had come to the show. They came with us on our bus to the venue, got them seated and went backstage to change and do our 'warm up'. We always had a room dedicated to do two or three songs to get in the right mood for the show. There was a simple drum kit, and a few Fender Twin amps. We would play upbeat songs like 'She Won't Dance With Me' and 'Sweet Little Rock 'n' Roller'. So the show started with 'Hot Legs' and all was going smoothly until 'Baby Jane' when I disappeared for a short time. Between the stage and the PA wings there was an enormous gap of about six feet, with no white tape at the edges to warn of impending doom. I strolled along to the front right of the stage and fell right through the gaping void, bouncing off the scaffolding on my way to the ground. It must have been about a ten foot drop. My guitar was smashed as was my transmitter, my shirt was ripped and I was cut up pretty badly. The first thing I thought was, 'I must get a tetanus shot.' It's so weird what one thinks of when the adrenaline is pumping through the body.

Anyway, I changed my shirt and guitar and managed to get back on stage before the end of the song. Rod told me later he was looking at me, turned away for a second and then noticed I had vanished. At the time he had no idea what had happened. After the show was finished he saw the cuts on my chest and arms and said, 'You'll carry those to your grave.' I believe it was another case of Azetta (my Guardian Angel) looking after me. Either that or the alcohol consumed before the show making me flexible. Or, perhaps a little of both! Notwithstanding, I was very lucky and did get a tetanus shot and a check-up the next morning. I was fine. The tour must go on! And on… and on…

Budapest was on the same tour. And, I think we were only the second 'western act' to play there. The first was Queen. We flew there on Aeroflot. The plane had an unusual seating arrangement, as some of the seats faced each other with a table between them. The cabin crew all looked like female shot putters and they weren't particularly pleasant. I remember when the meal was served my salad had a caterpillar in it. I showed it to the attendant who just looked at me and said, 'Well at least you know it's fresh,' and walked away. I would never fly on Aeroflot again! The plane was only carrying us, our equipment but no grand piano for Kevin. We were told that there would be one provided at the venue for us so nobody was really concerned.

Of course, when we got there, there was no piano. Panic time! Some research was done with the local promoter and we were told we would have one within the hour. Great. It turned out that four of the local crew were the Hungarian Olympic Wrestling team and were despatched to collect it. They went to the Symphony Hall, knocked on the door which was eventually opened by the one security guard and told him they were 'borrowing' the piano. He protested of course but they locked him in his office and told him that the piano would be returned by the end of the evening.

The piano turned up on the back of a fruit truck and the four of them hoisted it onto the stage and put it in place. It needed tuning from the bumpy ride but it all worked out in the end and was duly returned to the hall. I can't imagine that happening anywhere else.

Budapest is a beautiful city and we were staying at The Hyatt right on the river. The hotel was ok but there were some odd things about it. For example, the toilet paper holder in the bathroom had a lock on it so it couldn't be pilfered. They must have heard about our reputation. And the restaurant left a lot to be desired as well. Never mind, it was an adventure all the same. We had a few days off after the show and we were sent to what can only be described as a holiday camp for those who could afford it. It was a strange place but we made the best of it. Pretty soon we were off to civilisation again.

We arrived in Berlin and asked the taxi driver if there were any other bands in town. He told us that Kajagoogoo were there for a concert and told us where they were staying. Jim, Kevin and I went to their hotel while they were on stage.One of us went to the front desk and told them we were with the band and they gave us keys to two of the bedrooms. We moved everything that wasn't fixed into the bathroom and then folded the mattresses in two before we left so that they would jam the doors. Members of Kajagoogoo returned after the concert and couldn't get in to their rooms. We feigned total innocence and said we couldn't believe anyone could behave so immaturely. Two years later I bumped into one of the band and admitted it was us. He didn't seem to mind then... a lot of water under the bridge... and some of it poured into their beds.

While were we were in Berlin, we needed to cross into the East sector behind the Iron Curtain and I had left my passport in my hotel room. The border guard inevitably demanded to see my passport, but I didn't have it or any other identification on me. The aforementioned wardrobe mistress Louise showed him a newspaper photograph and a review of the concert we had just done – luckily with my name underneath. The official, initially suspicious, was immediately impressed and waved me through. I always believed that rock 'n' roll breaks down barriers and opens many doors, but this was unexpected!

Rod was always great on these tours – he kept everyone together. And was always up for a gag. During a US tour we had a couple of free days and our keyboard player John Corey (later of the Eagles and now of The Who) asked for time off. 'No problem,' said Rod and we told him to meet us at the next gig, which we said was Phoenix, Arizona. Of course, he turned up – only to find it was a Kenny Rogers show. In those days we didn't have what are now called 'road books', which map our schedule and itinerary (never mind mobile phones), so it made it hard for him to get in touch with us. Nonetheless, he did catch up with us at the right city at the right time, and I have to say he took it very well.

We had a saying on the road in those days; to ensure safe departure and arrival, 'NEVER leave the singer'. We were once playing in

Cincinnati and Jim Cregan was accompanied by his girlfriend, Adrianna. He told us he'd meet us at the airport at the 'General Aviation Gate', which was where the private plane was stationed. He was late (as usual) so Rod said, 'Let's go.' The door was closed and we were being pushed from our 'parking spot' when we suddenly see Jim and Adrianna running up to the gate. They managed to get through and ran on to the runway, and waved at the pilot to stop the plane. The pilot did just that and the two of them ran up the stairs and climbed aboard. As I said, 'NEVER leave the singer!'

Occasionally, if there were a couple of people who were late getting seated for the opening of the gig, Rod would stop the show and we would start the whole thing up again. They were always so embarrassed! Sometimes the singer would tell the audience where we were staying that night and loads of them would turn up. What he hadn't told them was that we weren't going to be there as we would sometimes fly out straight after the show. Most annoying for the unfortunate hotel and disappointing for the fans in retrospect, but I'm afraid to say at the time we found it amusing.

When I used to take the tube to school, on the walls of the platform at Earl's Court tube station, I used to see posters inviting people to emigrate to Australia, which advised that the Australian Government would pay for the boat passage, and give each emigrant ten pounds. I think those who wanted to go were termed, 'Ten Pound Poms'. This memory came flooding back the first time I went to Australia with Rod. After we landed, and were allowed to disembark, two men got on the plane with an aerosol in each hand and sprayed some sort of chemical all the way through the cabin. We all felt like the old convicts being showered with disinfectant. And going through passport control was not an easy task either. We were grilled as to why we were coming into the country even though the visas plainly showed that we were working there. None of us were given more than one day over the duration of the visit. Oh how times had changed.

Once when we were in Sydney, Wham were launching a record and staying in the same hotel. There was a party in the lounge, which Kevin Savigar, myself and our wives crashed. We were at the same table, talking to George Michael (another terrible loss), when he had to go and make his speech. Of course, while he was gone, we spiked his drink

– but I don't think he even noticed. We seemed to like spiking drinks in those days.

Oh… and just in case you were wondering about the chapter title, *Crudelis Sed Justi*, this was the motto/slogan we had emblazoned across specially made t-shirts for the band. The translation? 'Cruel but fair'. What else?

7

'MY BROTHER JAKE, HAT, SHADES, HEAD IN A DAZE'

July 2016 West Hollywood

Dear Jake,

Well, it's been some time since we last spoke to each other. There were ups and downs with us as I'm sure you remember, especially later in your life when you were consumed with that awful, awful drug heroin. I don't really blame you for that as you and I both know you were coerced into it by that girlfriend of yours at the time. I didn't like or trust her from the day I met her. I know you were so attached to her and she took advantage of that and dragged you into her terrible addiction. It's a weird thing about that particular drug – if someone is using it they feel a need to get someone else to experience the same high. There's not much more than a day I don't think about you, and how much I miss your dry sense of humour.

I left Rod's band in 1987, wanting to do something different and looking for another challenge. It had been a great experience recording and touring with him and so quitting was quite a hard decision to make but at the time I believed it was the right thing to do. I'd had a wonderful time – like being on holiday with mates and recording and playing the occasional gig, I had become tired of being on the road. I read in a newspaper, 'Not a good week for Rod Stewart, Kelly Emberg and Robin Le Mesurier have both left Rod.'

I had been good friends with members of the Pretenders – but sadly the band had suffered a double tragedy; James Honeyman-Scott had died five years previously, and Pete Farndon overdosed the following year. They were both wonderful people and it was so sad to lose them so young.

Anyhow, I called drummer Martin Chambers and suggested we put a band together. He was more than willing to oblige so we started working on finding a bass player and a singer. We eventually decided on a bass player, Alfie Agius who used to be in The Fix and a singer called Gary Lewis. We called ourselves 'The Committee'. We began rehearsing and I wrote some songs with Gary so that before long we had enough of a catalogue to go in the studio and record half a dozen tracks. We did the recordings at the Island Records studio in Chiswick, thanks to Martin's connection with The Pretenders and Chris Blackwell, who ran the record company. All seemed to be going swimmingly until Christmas Eve, when we thought we were about to sign a contract with Island Records, and Chris Blackwell rang to say he had changed his mind. There was to be no contract. What an awful Christmas present. Talk about no room at the inn.

I was going back and forth between London and LA for work, and still sorting out my green card application. After our rejection by Island, Martin and I decided to try our luck in LA. Gary left the band and so Alfie, Martin and I went to LA to find management and hopefully a record deal.

We did one showcase at the 'China Club' in LA which went well. There were lots of agents and reps from various record labels. An article in *Variety* stated that, if someone had dropped a bomb on the club that night, the whole of the LA record industry would have been wiped out. Sadly the band just didn't work out and we never recorded. I continued to work in LA as a session musician and I signed a songwriting deal with Sony, but my future was a little insecure.

Bun was back at work at The Playboy club, but before we met, she had worked with Peggy Honeyman-Scott, James' widow at the Rolling

Stones' London office as one of Mick Jagger's assistants and they had become good friends. Peg and Bun had the idea of putting together a book of recipes and personal photos of rock celebrities, including Mick Jagger, Ronnie Wood, Sting, Mick Fleetwood, Frank Zappa, Jeff Lynn and Grace Slick. Rick Nelson's *Nuclear Chicken Wings* and Fleetwood Mac's *Fiesta Dip* were just two of the featured dishes. Rod's recipe for a hangover sandwich was reviewed by someone who said, '… Rod looks like he needs to have one of his own sandwiches.' *Rock and Roll Cuisine* was published in November 1988 and had been quite successful so Bun wanted to do another one.

It was a difficult time for me because workwise I was trying to figure out what I was going to do next and I became a bit down and depressed. *Rock and Roll Cuisine* had been significant for Bun in that it was the first time she had been in the spotlight in her own right and not as a reflection of somebody else. She now felt more independent, confident about who she was, and had achieved something for herself.

So, Bun decided to return to Los Angeles to do a sequel to the cook book. Unfortunately the sequel to *Rock and Roll Cuisine* never happened, but more significantly this need for independence, somewhat ironically, led Bun into another relationship with musician and lyricist Paul Rafferty, while she was in California. Bun rang to tell me what had happened straightaway. She was very honest with me, but was racked with guilt.

That night I was with Jim Cregan at the Langham hotel, near BBC Broadcasting House for some kind of birthday bash for a friend. I was feeling pretty miserable and it obviously showed because right from the start, Jim kept asking me what was the matter, what was up with me, why was I so quiet? I was pretty uncommunicative and after about two hours of denying anything was wrong, I finally confessed that I was in a state because Bun had met someone else. I know it's ridiculous – but it did seem like a confession and I can only surmise that the reason it took me so long to tell Jim was because I was just so embarrassed. I found it difficult to open up to even to a dear friend.

It was a bit of a bombshell. But I wasn't angry. I don't really do angry. Wasting time and energy on something that you can't change is pointless. If I did or do ever get upset, I become very quiet and in those days I would lock myself away with a drink. Of course I was saddened but I wanted Bun to be happy and it was true that we had grown apart. Our relationship had shifted in the years we had been together – we had become more like brother and sister. And I suppose, selfishly, I simply just wanted to get on with my life and concentrate on playing and writing without any great feelings of bitterness or remorse to occupy me.

I can now see that this situation was so similar to what had happened to my mum and dad. Looking back I was reacting in a very similar way to how Dad had been when Mum had moved John Schofield into the family house and Dad had remained at Eardley Crescent. Dad never got angry – he just got on with his life, and so remained friends with Mum for the rest of her life. I was behaving in exactly the same way. Sigmund Freud would have had a ball with our family...

Of course Bun was really surprised by my stoicism. She told me later that if I'd shown a bit of fight and a bit of passion about her, she might have come back to me. I understand that my lack of emotion was frustrating and she didn't always know how I was feeling. But she also knew this was how I was and had always loved the fact that I was non-judgmental and my love for her had always been unconditional. I am the person I am – and hope that I am the same with everyone. We had been together for about twelve years, but were no longer in love. We'd become friends and we still are. We look out for each other... and always will.

Jake, remember when I came back to live in London for those few years and we shared the house Waterford Road? I found your stash and then tried hiding it. After you came home, you looked for it and you were in a complete panic. Eventually I told you that I had it and seeing you in such a state I just had to return it to you. I knew in my heart that you would fall apart without it. It was horrible to see you so distressed. I'll never forget it.

Jake and I had very different personalities when we were young kids. He was a clown – outgoing and a natural comedian who would do anything for attention whereas I was more introverted, shy and much more serious. Despite the fact that he was my younger brother – or perhaps

123

because he was – he was the show stealer and liked to have attention. This was sometimes difficult for me as I was more on the outside. But even so the two of us were extremely close. Jake had followed me to Sussex House but then attended Holland Park Comprehensive for his secondary schooling. Holland Park was actually one of London's first comprehensive schools and in those days a very trendy, progressive school with modern ideas and an egalitarian approach. According to the school's website, 'it attracted high profile socialist grandees and a smattering of literati and glitterati of West London'. And also my brother… Like me, Jake wasn't really interested in education, apart from when he went on to study music at Goldsmiths College in Deptford. And also like me, he was always interested in music. When I was much younger, I had a drum kit in our basement but I always found it easier to carry around a guitar – and it was simply an instrument with which I soon fell in love. At the age of ten, Jake started messing about on my kit which he soon mastered. He knew from the start that he wanted to be a percussionist and never swayed from it.

Jake was in various groups after leaving school including The Orb, and Central Line, worked with Roxy Music, wrote songs with Sade and one of his songs 'Fine Time' recorded by British singer Yazz made it into the top ten in the UK singles charts. The Dream Academy debut album by the group of the same name was released in 1985 and was produced by Pink Floyd's David Gilmour and Nick Claird-Clowes. The group featured the multi talented Guy Pratt – the album went to number 20 in the charts. In his book, *My Bass and Other Animals,* Guy Pratt later wrote, 'My first rehearsals with Dream Academy were in Nick Laird-Clowe's bedroom. I drafted in my mate Jake Le Mesurier to play drums. He was one of the funniest people ever to draw breath and a brilliant drummer.'

Guy's father was an actor and was a friend of Dad's and Joannie and Guy became a close friend of Jake's. They were housemates at Waterford Road for a while and used to frequent Ronnie Scott's together. They were once in the club to see Machito, the Afro-Cuban band leader and musician and Guy was picked from the audience onto the stage where he encouraged Machito to play one encore after another. Guy was woken the following morning by Jake, informing him that Machito had died that night, very soon after the performance, 'You know what you've done, Guy, you've only gone and killed the king of mambo.' That was typical of my brother.

Jake and I drifted apart in our teenage years when Jake became a bit of 'a lost soul' and there was a period in our late teens when we didn't see eye to eye – I guess there was inevitably some sibling rivalry but he was never jealous of my success. No, it was mainly that I didn't approve of some of his friends who I felt were a bit dodgy and not a good influence. The Andy Fraser/Paul Rodgers song that the iconic band Free recorded and gives this chapter its title, 'My Brother Jake' contains some prophetic and poignant lyrics.

Apart from the opening line used in the chapter title, the song continues, 'Have you thought about changing your ways... try making some friends... Jake it's not too late to start again... what's gone wrong with you, your candle is burning, the wheel's are turning, what you gonna do?' That's not to say that it was Jake's choice to get hooked on drugs – that's not the way it works. And he certainly had friends – but not many that I liked or of whom I approved. Other than smoking dope, he wasn't into drugs in such a big way until he met Janet, a New Yorker, who turned him on to heroin. Before her, he had a girlfriend, called Beatrice, who was killed in a car crash at the age of seventeen. He was the same age and inevitably this tragedy affected him deeply and it took him a few years to get over. I don't believe that is the reason why Jake became an addict – that's too simplistic, because he was always a party boy and liked to have fun and be adventurous.

I tried to get Jake off smack and told him it was going to kill him one day, but he simply told me, 'I can't come off it. I need it.' I suppose at least he was honest. But it was awful to see him strung out – he attained a sense of euphoria but then his character would change and would behave erratically. I'm lucky that I've never had a habit – in fact I've never wanted to take heroin. I saw what it did to other people.

Our wicked stepmother, Joannie had remained great friends with Bruce Copp, who was by now living in Barcelona. Joannie loved it so much that she decided she wanted to live there and she and Bruce decided to open a guest house in Sitges, an arty and very gay resort just 10 miles for Barcelona. 'Casa Antigua' was four hundred years old and full of beautiful old tiles. It was ideally situated in the heart of the town and close to the beach. The two of them knew so many people, particularly actors, performers and writers in London who they believed would want to spend some time in Spain.

During this time Jake was admitted to hospital in London with a mastoid infection, a middle ear infection. His addiction was starting to affect his health and he was living the typically chaotic lifestyle of an addict. Joannie came back from Spain and went to see Jake at St. Mary's hospital in Paddington with her son and David's then wife, Susie, 'When we saw him looking so frail lying in bed with tubes and drips attached to him, and his head bandaged, he held my hand... I had a talk with the ward sister about his condition. She told us that they knew that he had a habit, they had seen the track marks on his arms, that he was badly debilitated, and had lost the hearing in his left ear.'

> *Whilst you were in hospital for several weeks you had to lie flat, which must have been horrible. On one occasion I came to see you and you were recovering pretty well, although you told me you had lost most of your hearing in one ear. But I do remember you saying, 'If I have to listen to a stereo mix, I'll need to listen to it twice, one for stereo left the other time for stereo right!'*

The medical team had wanted to put Jake on a withdrawal program of methadone, but he refused this and instead chose to go 'cold turkey'. He was of the opinion that he might become dependent on methadone, which can happen. He thought he could kick his heroin habit without taking any substitute medication.

We had a family conference and I asked Joannie if she would consider taking him back to Sitges with her – it was a chance for him to be looked after properly and a new life away from all memories and temptations. We were trying to rescue him. This was a sort of intervention before they became popular in the treatment of addicts – a process where family members and friends remove the addict from home into some sort of rehab when the addict themselves don't realise the seriousness of their addiction or can't do anything about it.

Joannie offered him accommodation and employment as an odd job man in the guest house on the understanding that he had to 'stay clean'. She was adamant that she wasn't going to live with a junkie. However it was some weeks before Jake could be discharged – he was badly run down, and needed to be kept under medical supervision in case of a recurrence of his illness.

When Jake was eventually able to travel to Spain, he settled in well while being looked after by Joannie and Bruce, although he developed further infections in his mouth and throat and had trouble swallowing. He lived on soups and yoghurt, became very weak and lost a lot of weight.

Gradually, however, Jake's health improved and his sense of humour came back. I gave him a few hundred quid as a Christmas present and typically, he wanted to buy presents for everyone else with the money. He began to take more interest in the house, doing odd jobs. Joannie recalls that, 'He was good to have around, easy to live with as he became more relaxed and contented. He learned Spanish. I must say he was absolutely adorable during that time. Everyone loved him – particularly women as he was so very attractive.'

Bun and I stayed with Joannie in Sitges. It was so great to see Jake in good health and spirits. He took us to all of his favourite haunts in the town as in restaurants and more importantly the 'comfy bars' for drinks he loved to introduce us to. There was one bottle of something rather like tequila, but with a tiny lizard at the bottom of the bottle. Similar idea to the worm found in a particular mescal from Mexico. There are a couple of explanations for this; to test the alcohol content is just right – so if the worm is alive and wriggling it's too weak and if the worm dies – it's too potent. Another was that it gave the mescal more taste! Now, for the sake of tradition, they still put something that looks like a worm... but it's plastic. Anyway, this bottle was nearly empty so we finished it off when Jake dropped the reptile from the bottle on to the table and ate it! You could hear the bones crush as he was chewing it.

Despite all that, it was really good to see him, he still had his dry wit that he was known for and seemed to be very happy in Sitges. As we strolled round the town it was obvious he was loved by all the locals we ran into. For me I was very happy to connect with him again after such a long time not seeing him. He felt like a brother again – the brother I knew when we were growing up – not the person who I knew during his heroin induced days. He was someone quite different then.

During this time Jake was offered several recording contracts, but always refused to take these up. We didn't really know why – it's possible that returning to London's music scene would be too much for him in terms of his addiction. Joannie asked him if he felt he still needed drugs and Jake replied, 'No… not physically, my body has got over it, but I'd be lying if I said that I'm cured mentally, a junkie is never really cured, but I never want to go through that again. I was in so much pain in the hospital.' He managed to kick his habit in the physical sense but admitted the psychological dependency would always remain.

When you were in Sitges with Joannie, I remember a story she told me about an avocado which she was going to prepare as part of a salad for one of her guests. When she couldn't find it, you told her nonchalantly that you ate it. She was somewhat disappointed as it was the last one and she was also a little short of cash at the time, to which you replied, 'Joan, take a leaf out of my book and relax!' Typical you. I was so happy you were there and recovered and got 'clean' too. I was very proud of you. Plus you began writing music again.

One of my favourite haunts when I was travelling between Los Angeles and London and awaiting residency was Browns in Covent Garden. Jake knew one of the owners and so I used to hang out there regularly. One night I met Caron Keating, who at that time was a very popular presenter of the BBC's flagship children's television programme *Blue Peter*. We became good friends – Caron was absolutely lovely in every way – her character matched her looks and she spent a lot of time at Waterford Road. In fact, although she had been raised in Northern Ireland she had been born in Fulham and obviously felt at home in the neighbourhood.

In 1989, having bought Jake's share, I sold the house to Caron's mother Gloria Hunniford, also a television and radio presenter. Tragically, Caron was diagnosed with breast cancer and died at the age of forty-one in 2004, leaving a husband and two children. The Caron Keating Foundaton, a fund raising organisation, helping various cancer charities, was set up by Gloria and Caron's two brothers Paul and Michael. I am friends with them both – Michael still lives in Waterford Road and I stay there whenever I'm in London. The house is full of memories and I'm so pleased I still have a link with my old home.

Oh… and… I still treasure the *Blue Peter* badge that Caron gave me!

I was going back and forth between London and Los Angeles during this time and although I had split with Bun, we remained close. After all that time seeing her again, it was fine, no feelings of animosity and in fact the first time I moved back, for a while, I did stay with her. But this wasn't easy in the circumstances and I needed to be on my own. At one point I was sharing a house with an old friend called Hein Hoven. Hein was in the music business as a producer and jingle writer, and very successful. His girlfriend at the time was Sharon Stone who was charming and very friendly. At that time she was making *Total Recall* with Arnold Schwarzenegger and I remember she described a scene in which she had to beat him up. I still see her occasionally. Hein moved back to Europe many years ago.

I met Joanne Russell when Rod started going out with Kelly Emberg and we had an instant connection. Jo was with the same modelling agency as Kelly and they were both thick as thieves. Jo was originally from Manchester and left the UK to model in Europe and then in New York. Jim Cregan and Jo were good mates and whenever the band were in town or on tour somewhere we would meet up with Jo, who enjoyed hanging out with us. She recently explained, 'They all made me feel welcome. And I remember everyone seemed like a big family, teasing each other and making fun of each other as only the Brits can do sometimes! I'd get quite homesick and when I spent time with them it felt less so. Plus we were all in the same kind of boat travelling all over the world so often we'd end up in the same place together.'

Jo was living in LA soon after the time that Bun and I split up and was coincidentally looking for a roommate. She was renting a property and offered me the second bedroom. I was so grateful for the offer and I moved in – purely as friends. I was still pretty devastated by the breakup and Bun was happy that I had somewhere comfortable and secure to stay because she was worried about me. I think it alleviated her guilt a little. Bun and Jo were also good friends which helped.

The house we rented was described as 'a boathouse', although it wasn't anywhere near water! It was an 'A framed' building the front of which was on stilts on Woodrow Wilson Drive, overlooking a canyon on Mulholland Drive in The Hollywood Hills. I wondered how it would fare in an earthquake as LA is actually built on the San Andreas fault line and susceptible – as I found to my cost after that night at Le Dôme – to regular strong tremors. It wasn't long until we found out. Within about a month of being there we had quite a noticeable quake one afternoon and we both ran outside rather sharpish. Although the house shook and swayed quite a lot, there was actually no damage. It turned out that the stilts descend sixty feet into the bedrock so that these particular houses are incredibly robust. In fact, when we had the very bad quake in '94, not one of the houses that were built on stilts actually collapsed.

Jo recalls, 'I loved living with Robin. He cooked and I didn't so that was a plus! And he was so clean and tidy! We had great conversations and liked many of the same things. He put up with all manner of people that hung out there and we had some really fun times. When the lease on Woodrow Wilson was up we decided to look for another house together because we got along so well.' We moved to a house on Wonderland Avenue just off Laurel Canyon in the Hollywood Hills. The street was infamous as the site of the Chandleresque termed 'Four on the Floor Murders' a few years previous when four members of the drug dealing Wonderland gang were beaten to death. Their murders remain unsolved although the attack was allegedly masterminded by nightclub owner Eddie Nash. The whole nasty business was very LA as another suspect was porn star John Holmes, who was arrested, tried and acquitted. Holmes was infamous for having the most extraordinary sized… well… all I can say is that Rod would not have been able to fit a drawing of it in a normal sized passport.

Anyway the house Jo and I shared on Wonderland Avenue had originally been built as a hunting lodge in the 1920s, just. It was modelled on the house that the Seven Dwarfs lived in, in the *Snow White* Disney movie. It was very quaint with a brook running through the end of the garden and quite unique. The situation was beautiful – very peaceful and quite rustic, but not far from the street life that I need. It was very cosy, although I occasionally felt uneasy and was convinced that there was someone or something else in the house. Jo's parents visited from England and also felt a presence in that house. Luckily we didn't know about the 'Wonderland murders' at that time!

It was around that time that Jim Cregan was producing an album for The London Quireboys, who were managed by Sharon Osbourne. I played on most of the album, which we recorded at Cherokee Studios in West Hollywood. Jo fell madly in love with the band's singer, 'Spike' (Jonathan Gray) who was a lovely bloke, very good looking and loved a drink or two! I was going out with a girl called Pat Lalama, who was one of the 'Anchors' on Fox News and is now an Emmy award winning investigative journalist. Pat was and is very smart and I admired her intellect. She lived in an apartment right underneath Axl Rose, which as you can imagine wasn't the quietest of spots. Sadly Jo broke up with Spike and was heartbroken. I was still licking my wounds after the split with Bun and Pat and I didn't last that long together. Luckily Jo and I had each other for support and friendship.

We only leased the house for a year or so and had lots of wonderful dinner parties in the large circular dining room. Johnny Depp used to come by occasionally for tea before he went off to audition for one part or another. Of course, this was a very long time before he became a 'Pirate'. I threw Jo a 30th birthday party there. It was a great bash with many friends and the guests included Elmer Valentine, who co-founded the most famous clubs in LA, Ric Ocasek from The Cars and his wife, model Paulina Porizkova, Nicholas Cage and Sarah Jessica Parker. I didn't know who SJP was in those days, as it was way before *Sex in the City*, but she was lovely. The party went into the wee hours and most likely there was a lot of tidying up before we retired. I can't bear to wake up to a mess the following day.

I always tell my American friends that the British celebrate July 4th (Independence Day) because it's the day the UK got rid of the USA! On one of these holidays, Jo and I decided to dress up, me in drag wearing one of her wigs and some of her clothes, and her attired like a hooker. We met some friends at a place on Sunset Boulevard, something akin to and English pub called The Coach and Horses. There was much imbibing and I stood on the bar, looked at myself in the mirror and said, 'I quite fancy myself.' As we were leaving, waiting for a taxi, a car pulled up by the curb. Jo walked over and said, 'Can I help you?' I immediately dragged her away as I'm sure the driver though she was looking for a client. And he probably thought I was another hooker…

Jo and I did have much fun together, but eventually I felt I needed to be living alone and Jo still maintains I needed some peace and quiet!

Jo was younger than me, some of her friends were even younger and we were at different stages in our lives. Jo had also co-written a children's book that was about to be published and moved to a house that she owned in upstate New York. She still lives there and has an eleven-year-old daughter. Jo and I remain close friends to this day.

I then moved to an apartment on Fountain Avenue in West Hollywood, where, funnily enough, I had a similar 'ghostly' experience. It was a beautiful two storey 1930s Mediterranean style building with a lovely garden and a fountain in the middle. But, something very strange happened there. I often used to catch a glimpse of something moving very fast across from my bedroom to my studio. I thought nothing of it… but here is the really weird thing… one evening I was sitting on the corner of my bed watching television and channel surfing when I suddenly felt as if a large cat or dog had jumped on the bed behind me. It gave me quite a start. I looked behind me and was even more surprised to see a large indentation on the bed covers! It didn't really bother me but I was slightly alarmed and went back to the TV wondering what on earth had happened. That's the only time I've witnessed something of that nature. I think whatever the being was, it was trying to scare me out of the building! But it didn't and I went to bed that night without a care in the world.

I was in LA when I got the call to fly to New York for the audition for a Vodka Collins tour. I first met the multi instrumentalist Alan Merrill around 1979 or 1980 soon after The Arrows had split up. He was then with Runner, a band that recorded for Island and also an ATV Music Staff songwriter. We enjoyed a very boozy evening – all on the ATV Music expense account. We lost touch for years until Alan played guitar with Meat Loaf in the mid 1980s, and was touring England. We caught up again after the Reading Festival at Browns in 1988 when we discussed forming a trio with Martin Chambers. The following year, Alan's old Tokyo based band Vodka Collins was to have an unofficial reunion and tour of Japan and the drummer, the late Hiroshi Oguchi asked Alan to find a great guitar player for the project. According to Alan, 'he asked me to find someone who could play like Ron Wood, Eric Clapton and Jeff Beck. Plus the guitar player had to be good looking and slim! Not an easy order to fill. But I immediately thought of Robin and came to New York a couple of days later to rehearse Montana Studios with us for what would be the Vodka Collins Practise of Silence reunion tour of Japan.'

Hiroshi Oguchi was notorious. Once a conceptual artist and later turned actor and fashion designer, he was like the Keith Richards of Japan, heavily into drugs, alcohol and the rest. But a lovely guy. I went to New York for a couple of days to audition for the tour and after a couple of songs I was told, 'You're going to work out very well.' Nepotism at its best. A couple of weeks later I was on a plane to Tokyo to start rehearsals for the tour. There were quite a few Americans in the band, three blonde (naturally – if not natural) backup singers, from the group Kid Creole and The Coconuts, Alan, and an American bass player. The rest of the group, keyboards and horns, were Japanese. My guitar tech hardly spoke a word of English and my Japanese is limited to 'please' and 'thank you' (my parents would have been proud of my manners – even in Japanese). But it worked out fine with the tech – he was great at his job. After the rehearsals we were on the road playing all the major venues in Japan. It was very successful and a good time was had by all. Funnily enough, The US Immigration service granted me a letter of parole to do that tour. It was incredible that they would give me one to work but not to attend the funeral of my father! I guess, looking back, Alan was one of the first westerners to achieve pop cult status in Japan and he is still making great music. Unfortunately the same can't be said for Oguchi, who died from cancer in Tokyo in 2009.

Another favourite work memory was around 1991 when I got a call to make another record with Rod – this time being produced by Trevor Horn and engineered by Steve MacMillan. We were to record in Ireland at a beautiful sprawling old house in County Wicklow, a little south of Dublin. The studio was set up in the huge drawing room, in which there was plenty of room for us, our gear and the recording equipment. The album was to be called *Rod Stewart, Lead Vocalist* and featured David Palmer on drums, Carmine Rojas on bass, Kevin Savigar on keyboards, me and the brilliant Jeff Golub on guitar. Jeff sadly died in 2015.

It was a fabulous place in which to reside and record. We had a great time and even had a wonderful resident chef! I think we were there for about a month or so and occasionally we would venture out to the local village for a pint or two of Guinness or 'The Dark Stuff' as it was known locally. Surprisingly, we never were hassled by anyone, as

I think the locals were just glad to have us there. After that album I used to work with Trevor and Steve in LA for Rod's various albums. They were always fun to do. They reminded me of working with Mickey Most as in spending quite some time just chatting, recording a little and chatting more. The other fun part of working with Trevor was that Lol Crème (from 10 CC), was quite often in the studio with us, just hanging out. Lol is a lovely bloke and the pair of them were quite fond of weed so there was a lot of laughing during those sessions.

> *But, there was that fateful day when you met her in a bar. I still don't know her name… another addict. There is something very dark about addicts who seem to latch on to others who are, or recovering. Almost like some kind of dark magnetism.*

Sadly all was not now going well in Sitges. Jake's demeanour and behaviour had changed. Bruce Copp wrote in his autobiography, *Out of the Firing Line into the Foyer,* 'our lovely gentle and good natured Kim (Jake) became surly and uncommunicative. We searched his room when he was out and found needles and all his drugs paraphernalia. Joan confronted him and admitted that he had gone back on the junk. He apologised but insisted it was just a temporary lapse.'

Jake moved out of the guest house and into a flat in a seedy area of Barcelona with his new girlfriend. He used to ask Joannie and Bruce for money and they naturally did all they could to help him and give him food, but 'he looked like a ghost and it was obvious he was shooting up. We knew some of the funds were being used for drugs, but what could we do?'

In 1991 Joannie returned home to Ramsgate as her mother was ill and while she was there her granddaughter Emma Malin, then aged about ten and now an actress and writer, received a phone call to say that Jake had died. Jake had been spotted by friends in a Barcelona bar, crying and clearly distressed. Some hours later he was discovered in his flat with a needle in his arm and a large amount of heroin in his body. All his instruments and demo tapes had been stolen. It was 6th October – exactly the eleventh anniversary of Hattie's death and he was aged just thirty-five.

The day before Mum died, Jake had an argument with her. That affected him really badly throughout his life. There was some suspicion that racked with guilt, he killed himself, but I don't believe that. Jake always felt miserable on the anniversary of Mum's death and my feeling is that his girlfriend at the time wanted him to feel better and gave him too much smack. It's strange that he died on the 11th anniversary of Mum's death but I believe that was just a coincidence and that the overdose was an accident. But whatever the reason, it was a tragedy.

I was still sharing the house with Jo in Wonderland Avenue when Joannie called me. I felt helpless – I was so far away. It came as a complete shock, although he had been clean for a while I always knew that deep down 'once an addict always an addict' was a something of a truism and his addiction was such that it had been too much for him to kick completely.

Jim Cregan found out about Jake and insisted that we spend the day together. He lived nearby and made sure I didn't spend the whole day just drinking and wanted to occupy me. We went to the top of the Hollywood Hills and drove as far as we could on Mulholland Drive till it ended and you either have to go to the valley or towards the Pacific Ocean. We spent a long time at the beach with me mostly reminiscing about Jake and Jim asking questions about him. He was incredibly understanding and comforting. I shed a few tears, but we also laughed at some of Jake's shenanigans through the years.

We came back to Wonderland Avenue and Jim stayed well into the evening when we had a couple of drinks. Jo was there too and was incredibly supportive. It suddenly occurred to me that I had no immediate family left except Joannie and my cousin John-Paul Jacques, my Uncle Robin's son. I felt somewhat adrift. The thought of not hearing Jake's wit and sarcasm any more was unbearable. I didn't realize how much I missed him until he was gone. But he left a great legacy. Every time I get the chance to visit Joannie we always talk about him as if he was still with us. I believe he is in a way. There was a wake in Ramsgate and his ashes are buried next to Dad's in St George's Church in the town.

Even after your death there was some humour… When David, (Joannie's Son) went to collect your ashes, there was some confusion about your given name of Kim. So, instead of 'Jake

Charles Le Mesurier'... the label on the urn read 'King Charles Le Mesurier.'

You were a great inspiration to so many people. I'm proud of you and miss you dearly. Robin. X

My brother 'Jake'.

8

FOOL FOR THE BLUES

My first encounter with the legendary record producer Phil Spector occurred on my birthday in 1992. I had decided to have some friends over for a bit of a bash at my apartment on Fountain Avenue in West Hollywood. Not a huge gathering or a wild event as I had been invited to a listening party for Ronnie Wood's latest album *Slide on This* at the A&M studio later that evening. So the party was for just a few close friends, including Ronnie. We couldn't party too long as some of us needed to leave for A&M. Ronnie was the first to leave for the studio and on exiting told me, 'Get there soon as you can.' No problem. Only a couple of us were driving as I knew there would be much imbibing during the night. When I got there it was already in full swing, the album being played over and over between other music. It was a really well organised soirée with a great bar and lots of nibbles. There were also lots of friends I hadn't seen for a while including dear Mac (Ian McLagan).

The night seemed to go on for ages and much jollity was had by all. At about three or so in the morning I decided it was time for me to leave. Now the studio where the playback took place is very large and I was looking everywhere to say goodnight to Ronnie and Mac. I couldn't find them anywhere until I was told they were in a little makeshift room within the studio made from gobos (sound isolation walls). I found it easily and as I opened the door and entered the room Spector was standing by the wall to my right. He immediately reached into the inside of his jacket, pulled out a gun and pointed the snub-nosed revolver directly in my face. I didn't scream or duck, I just stood there motionless. I was glued to the floor and more than a little freaked out. The next thing I heard was Ronnie shouting, 'No, no, put that away, he's a friend of mine.' The gun was lowered and I looked at Spector – a short, ugly, little shite with a mean look. It was the scariest moment of my life. He slowly and begrudgingly put it back in his jacket and my relief was huge. I ignored him and went to say my goodbyes to Ronnie and Mac.

Some years later Spector was charged with the murder of Lana Clarkson, whom I knew. She was a hostess at The House of Blues, a music venue on Sunset Boulevard within walking distance of my home on Fountain Avenue. I used to see her whenever I went there. She was a charming girl and always very friendly. Eventually he was brought to trial in 2007 and after weeks of testimony a mistrial was declared due to a hung jury. He was quoted as saying that Lana's death was an 'accidental suicide, and that she 'kissed the gun'.

Sometime in 2008 I got an email from the district attorney in LA asking to have a meeting with me. At first I was a little worried as to why the DA wanted to talk to me. I ignored the request for the first few days but Jules convinced me to answer her – as she said, I hadn't done anything wrong and had nothing to hide. So I called her. Her name was Elizabeth Devine and she told me that she had read an article in a newspaper from the UK about how Phil Spector had drawn a gun on me at A&M. I actually had no idea it had ever been reported in the press.

Ms Devine he told me that there was to be a re-trial in the Lana Clarkson case and asked me if I could talk to her about what happened to me. I was relieved and agreed to tell her whatever she wanted to know – at least whatever I could answer. We made a date for her to come and talk to me and a few days later she came to the house with a partner, another female agent. They were both armed with guns, which was a little intimidating to say the least, but they were both very calm and sensible and made me feel comfortable.

Ms Devine told me this interview would only take about fifteen minutes or so although they actually stayed for about two hours! I recounted the story at A&M, and how it scared me. I was reluctant to testify, but the fact that I knew Lana pricked my conscience. When they were preparing for the retrial they eventually asked me, 'If Lana was your sister or daughter, would you be prepared to take the witness stand?' In an instant I said, 'Yes, of course I would.' Thankfully I was never called, as I didn't want to see that little bastard again. Spector was tried again for second-degree murder on 20th October 2008 and six months later the jury this time found Spector guilty of murdering Clarkson. He was sentenced on 29th May 2009 to 19 years to life in state prison.

I was in illustrious company. At various times, since he had become obsessed with firearms in the late 1950s, Spector had allegedly waved various weapons at John Lennon, Leonard Cohen and Debbie Harry. His treatment of his wife Ronnie is well documented, keeping her hostage at their mansion and regularly threatening her. I heard that Spector was in Keith Richards' suite at a hotel in New York at some point and pissed off Keith so much that Keith warned him, 'There are two ways out of here, the window or the door. Take your pick!' Spector took a swift exit.

It made me think how easy it is to buy guns and assault weapons in the USA and so consequently I'm all for gun control. The trouble is, The NRA, (National Rifle Association) have so much support and lobbying power that it is, sadly, an uphill battle. They always bring up the Second Amendment, which is the right to bear arms. Now this was written in 1791 for raising a militia and when it took two minutes to load a musket. Enough said.

I finally got the green light for my green card around Christmas 1993. I had received great support from Rod's management and Bun, who refused to divorce me until I was given residency, kept up the pretence that we were happily living together and even wrote to Bill Clinton pleading my case. The happy day that I went to Immigration and Naturalization Service, the official who I usually dealt with wasn't in the office and her replacement looked at my files which were about twelve inches thick and simply said, 'Well, Mrs Reed isn't here today so I'm going to grant you your permanent residency. Congratulations.' It had taken thirteen years, four or five separate applications and cost in the region of $100,000 in legal fees from when I first applied.

Chris Kimsey has been hugely influential on my career. Chris is an incredibly experienced engineer and producer who had worked with the Stones, Yes and Emerson Lake and Palmer before we even met and has since worked on hundreds of albums in various guises. He is now at the state of the art Olympic Studios where he started off and has actually designed the sound system for the studios' two cinemas.

We originally met through Paul Rafferty, but Chris knew of my work with Farm Dogs. Chris first met Johnny Hallyday when he was about eighteen and working at Olympic and had gone on to record about five albums with him. Johnny was a huge star in France – an icon for his singing and acting – but had never been that well known Stateside and was now desperate to record an album in English to crack the US market. Chris called me one day and asked me if I would write a couple of songs for this latest venture. Johnny also wanted a non French guitarist and Chris had immediately thought of me. I could perform a dual role.

Chris was now in LA and had booked Johnny Hallyday into the Marquis hotel (where we'd filmed 'Tonight I'm Yours' over a decade ago) and where he was also staying. I went down to meet them and Johnny and I clicked immediately – in fact I would describe him as a soul mate from day one. Johnny confirmed that he wanted me on board. Chris stayed on the Marquis – only to come down to reception a couple of days later and discover that Johnny had checked himself out. Apparently he wanted something a little less rock and roll and a little more classic Hollywood – somewhere more frequented by movie stars.

I wrote two tracks, 'Are the chances gone?' and 'Fool For The Blues' (lyrics by Paul Rafferty) for the album, which was titled *Rough Town*. The reader may wonder how I was able to work with Paul who had become involved with Bun, especially with the content of lyrics, which are reproduced at the end of the chapter, but I had no problem whatsoever writing with Paul. I certainly didn't see him as 'the enemy' and Paul certainly didn't seem to have a problem with me and was quoted as saying, 'As with most things with Robin it was a breeze, he's a joy to write with and very patient.' In fact we became good friends and still are to this day.

We recorded *Rough Town* at Ocean Way Recording studios on 6050 Sunset Boulevard. For a while the building became known as East West studios but more recently was renamed as United Recording Studios. Some formidable musicians were brought in for the session: Richie Hayward and Bill Payne both from the wonderful Little Feat and another drummer Ian Wallace of King Crimson fame. There was Colin James' a great guitarist from Canada, Hutch Hutchinson on bass and Chuck Leavell on keyboards, ex-Allman Brothers, and who has been with The Stones for many years. Chris Kimsey was really easy to work with and later reported, 'Johnny has a way of looking at someone who he likes or is impressed by – a wonderful expression, like a small child in admiration. I saw him look at Robin during that first recording and could see from the beginning that their relationship was going to work.' Chris has a fab sense of humour, which is always a positive with me. In fact Johnny does too, so it was an all round easy going session. All in all recording my first album with Johnny was a great experience.

After the album was finished, not only did the record company ask Chris and I to put a new group together for Johnny to promote the record in France. It does seem strange now that there were no plans to tour The US or The UK, as the purpose of the album was to attract an English speaking audience, but surprisingly I don't think it was even talked about at the record label. Foolish perhaps, but it's all moot now.

Johnny also asked me to take on the role of musical director for the *Rough Town* tour. Quite an honour. Johnny was very flattering and later said, 'Robin has worked with the best. The first time I saw him was when he was playing with Rod in Cannes. I wanted him in the band as soon as he had recorded on my album and written some songs. We got on straightaway. He and I are like an old married couple. There is a bond between us.'

The group consisted of Tim Moore and Jim Prime, piano/synths and Hammond B3 respectively, Ian Wallace, drums, Phil Soussan, bass, Ian Wilson, backup vocals and Phil Palmer and myself on guitars. They were a great bunch and we all got on very well. We all met up in Paris in the autumn to rehearse for about four weeks before starting the tour. The record company put us up in a shabby hotel in Pigalle, a sort of seedy area in Paris and I asked Caroline Molko, the record company executive, 'Why are we staying here?' She replied, 'Well this is where all the artists lived and worked.' I said, 'Painters, not musicians.'

We soon got moved to a Hilton, near The Eiffel Tower, which was much better all round! It wasn't going to be a very lengthy tour as it was only really a promo for the album. The first show was to be in Toulon in the south of France, not that far from where Johnny had a beautiful home, called *Lorada*, near St Tropez. Ian and I stayed there whilst we did production rehearsals in Toulon. Johnny used to breakfast on beer and a packet of Gitanes and needed a lot of coaxing to start rehearsing.

Anyway, it came to the day of the first show. We were at the gig doing last minute sound checks. Suddenly, Guy Marseguerra, who was the stage and crew manager at the time, came running down the backstage hallway in a panic and called out, 'Johnny's coming, Johnny's coming!' I wasn't quite sure what I was meant to do and so I just looked at him and said, 'Great.' I had got to know him quite well by staying with him and wasn't yet in awe of him. I only really knew him as a singer, albeit a great singer and I had never realised quite how revered he was, but I soon came to understand how much he was loved by the French, Swiss, Belgians and anywhere French is spoken.

The tour was to finish in Paris at an old music hall called La Cigale. Because it was such a small spot, there was a rumour going around his fan base that Johnny only played huge venues to crowds numbering anywhere between 20-80,000 people, and wasn't actually going to appear at this show. According to hearsay, an impersonator had been employed in his place. All nonsense, of course. It was a lovely gig, although funnily enough I get more nervous in intimate settings than playing to huge crowds. My confidence was boosted, however, when I saw a sign suspended from the balcony close to me, stage right that read 'Fool for Johnny' and I felt quite touched by this homage to my song.

I was now a permanent part of Johnny's band, playing and as MD (that's Musical Director – not Doctor of Medicine). The next tour was to be a lengthy seven month affair, and back to performing at huge venues. In Paris we did twenty-one shows at Bercy (an indoor sports arena and concert hall in the 12th arrondissement of Paris, which seats an audience of 18,000. I later told Don Henley of the Eagles that we sold out every night there and he almost fell out of his chair. The Eagles performed there for one night…

We were doing production rehearsals there and realised we didn't have a hairdryer in the dressing room. An absolute must as one can be soaked with sweat at the end of a show. I was standing on the stage with Guy, and told him we needed a hair dryer. He said, 'We can't afford one.' I drew his attention to the massive set, sound and lights, the 'B'

Fools for the Blues. That's me and Johnny Hallyday (MICHEL ANGELLI)

stage and said, 'You have to be kidding.' He saw my expression and said, 'Don't worry, we'll get one for you.' Sure enough, the next day one was supplied. Thank you, Guy!

There were so many dates over those months. In a week we would do four or five shows so it became a kind of blur as to where we were from time to time. One night Johnny came up to me and asked where we were. (Those were the days when we didn't have 'in ear monitors', which are moulded to your ears and block out everything except the mix you need). I told him I had no idea. A song or so later I looked at the back of the hall only to see Clermont Ferrand painted in huge letters. I went up to him and pointed to the back of the venue. He laughed and said, 'Thanks.' Just after we finished the song he said, 'Bon soir Clermont Ferrand.'

Following that experience, at the next show and all those after, the name of the city was on the teleprompter at the opening of the show. It was during that tour that Jim Prime left halfway due to 'personal difficulties'. That kind of put me in a bind as I was still MD and had to find an organ player the next day. I suddenly remembered that Ian Kewley, a great player who was in Stryder and Limey with me, was living in the South of France, and fortunately very close to where we were appearing next.

I managed to get hold of Ian, and we were very lucky as he'd just returned back from London a couple of days before. When he arrived we sat in the bus for three or four hours and crammed him with details about the show. When it came to the gig he did amazingly well considering how much he'd just had to ingest. As the tour continued, he became more and more comfortable with us and I was really happy with him. Johnny was also grateful for finding someone who could fill the gap so well.

It was around this time that I fell in love again. I met Brogan Lane at a party Kelly Emberg was giving at her house close to Manhattan Beach, just south of Los Angeles. Brogan had been Dudley Moore's third wife and I soon became completely besotted with her. She was wondrously tall and had this amazing smile. I felt an immediate attraction to her and, after chatting together for some time, I asked her if I could call her. I didn't waste time and rang her the next day and invited her out for dinner.

We saw each other quite a lot. I used to love to cook for her at her home, a beautifully decorated house in Toluca Lake, just over the hill in the San Fernando Valley. I say the house was beautiful because when I met her she had given up acting and was working as an interior designer. I used to see her as often as I could because later on that year I knew I would be back on the road with Johnny and I loved her very much. It was another long tour, but we kept in touch and when the tour was over towards the end of '95, we carried on happily where we had left off and spent that Christmas together. But just before Easter she called and asked if she could come to my house as she had something to tell me. I was intrigued but a little nervous at the same time.

Brogan told me that she couldn't commit anymore to our relationship. She said she just wasn't ready. I was gobsmacked... and completely heartbroken. It just so happened a short while after we split up, Joannie was going to be in Hawaii. I decided to meet them there just to get away and try and forget the hurt. It was great to see Joannie – she can be so understanding and philosophical about life. She helped me heal.

In 1995, I was recording with Rod again for his album *A Spanner in the Works*. We recorded it with a mobile at his house in LA. I co-wrote one of the tracks, 'Delicious' with Rod and Andy Taylor from Duran Duran. It didn't turn out to be quite so 'Delicious' because neither Rod nor I received any royalties from the song because Andy asked for 37 ½%, which was totally unfair and created a legal wrangle. So the royalty on the mechanicals (the sales) have been in limbo and held by Warner Bros since then. Sometimes I hate record companies... I've tried everything I can to get Andy to reach a compromise, but to no avail. He's impossible to track down. So, if you're reading this Andy...

A happier recording experience took place the same year, when we recorded the *Lorada* album at Johnny's eponymous house. The main living room was cleared of the furniture and all the amps, drums and keyboards were set with isolation walls. There was a mobile recording truck outside the house. It was also decided that we should use the ear monitors whilst recording, but unfortunately they were very rudimentary and difficult to work with. It was produced by Jean-Jacques Goldman, a great artist in his own right, who had also written a number of big hits for Johnny and other French artists. I got on with him very well, personally and professionally. However, after about a week working on the record, it really wasn't working out well because of technical difficulties, so we all moved to Paris to record it at Guillaume Tell, a great studio in Suresnes, just north of central Paris, which had been beautifully converted from an old theatre. It all went very smoothly there and the album was a great success.

The following year we were off again on the road on another long tour and it involved an interesting start for me and Phil Soussan. Johnny invited us to stay at Lorada for a few days before the start of the rehearsals and then towards the end of July we left Los Angeles for Paris, and changed planes for a flight to Nice. When we got there was a helicopter waiting for us to take us directly to his house. Yes, there was a helipad there… and within two hours we were on a boat, anchored in the Mediterranean enjoying a late lunch and dining on sea urchins fished up from the sea floor! Quite a trip, to say the least.

It was a great tour, which ended on 'Labor Day', an American holiday which falls on the first Monday in September. Bun called me when I got home and asked if I'd like to have dinner at Le Petit Bistro. She told me that Billy Francis was going to be there and I agreed to the plan as Billy was always good value. Also I've found that the best thing you can do to cope with jet lag is to stay up as long as possible. Bun had also invited along a woman called Jules, a friend of hers. Bun still felt a little responsible for me and wanted me to find happiness with someone else. She described Jules as 'really pretty and fun' and saw her friend as a future partner for me. This was so reminiscent of my parents and how my mum wanted my dad to be with Joannie over thirty years previously. I found out later that Jules really didn't want to go out that night and at that time had no interest in becoming romantically involved with someone new. Jules, born and bred in LA, worked in the fashion industry and had only just returned from Paris. She reluctantly agreed to go as a favour to Bun, but not to eat – just for a quick drink. She later recounted, 'I didn't have a chance. I was cornered into it.'

Bun made sure that we were sitting next to each other and Jules and I hit it off immediately. The next day I arranged to see her for lunch in downtown LA where she worked and we were soon inseparable. About five months into our relationship, we decided to take a holiday to Ixtapa in Mexico, a little fishing village with a great hotel on the top of a cliff overlooking the ocean. We had a wonderful time there and often ate out in various charming places in the village. There was one restaurant that was particularly great where a waiter would place a bottle of tequila on the table as soon as we sat down (NOT the stuff from the Eddie V H shoot!). The staff were lovely and at the end of the meal they worked out a rough estimate of how much we drank. And, it was very reasonable to boot.

When we arrived back in LA, I dropped Jules off at her house near my apartment in West Hollywood, only to find out that she had been burgled while we were away. They took almost everything; watches, jewellery, expensive luggage and almost everything she owned. We found her bedroom TV at the bottom of the stairs – perhaps they were scared off. Jules thought she knew who committed the crime but it couldn't be proved.

Jules was fearful about staying alone in her apartment and I agreed that she could live with me until she found somewhere else to live. But I soon realised that I didn't want her to find somewhere else to live and told her I wanted her to stay. She did and she's still with me – twenty years later.

In the early 90s, Stephanie Hyams, who later became Stephanie Taupin, and was originally *the Maître D'* at Le Dôme, had opened her own restaurant on Melrose Ave in West Hollywood. Cicada was a fantastic place, and very hip without even trying. Once a week she would have a group playing live in the large back room. Somehow or other I was asked to play with a girl called Meredith Baxter, a local singer/songwriter. She had a band but was looking for a guitarist. We met, played a little and I liked her style of music. I joined her group and we used to play at Cicada regularly. Bernie Taupin, who I've known for years, was always in attendance. One night, when we were having a drink after the gig, he pulled me to one side and asked me if I would like to work with him on a new project he wanted to put together. Naturally, I jumped at the chance to work with one of the greatest lyricists alive.

Thus began many meetings about the project. He wanted to have Dennis Tufano on board – they'd worked together before and Dennis was the singer in a quite successful group called The Buchanans in the seventies. Bernie asked me who we should have for another guitarist. Inevitably the first person that came to mind was Cregan. Jim had done a thirteen week US tour with Family, who were then supporting Elton John and so no formal introductions were required.

The best of times with Farm Dogs Left to right – Cregan (again)
Bernie Taupin, Dennis Tufano and 'the author' (CHRIS CUFFARO)

We had a group! Bernie found a very talented recording engineer/
co-producer called David Cole and suggested that we work at his ranch
in Santa Ynez, about a two hour drive north of LA near Santa Barbara,
California. Bernie's was a working ranch with cutting horses, which are
the horses that are trained to separate cows from the larger herd. We
used to rehearse and record in beautiful surroundings in the company
of Stephanie and lots of fine wines and tequilas. These were some of

my best times and I look back on those days with nothing other than pure affection and pleasure.

We had a daily ritual after breakfast of going to 'El Rancho Market' in Santa Ynez to buy food and wines for dinner. It's an exceptional shop with an incredible variety of great tequilas, wine and locally sourced vegetables and meat. We all had a part in the prep and cooking. Most evenings Daphne, Bernie's mum, who lived in a nearby cottage, would come up to the main house and have one or two cocktails that I had prepared for her. Daphne was an amazing woman; petite, incredibly knowledgeable and a joy to be with. She always used to find clippings from the press that pertained to my parents or me. She was a great part of my 'Farm Dogs' experience. Sadly she passed away on 19th November 2016, and will sorely be missed by me and all who came in contact with her.

The gym was turned into a studio which had a fabulous location overlooking the ranch below. The writing and recording was such an effortless procedure. Bernie already had a stack of lyrics for about thirty songs and all Jim and I had to do was put the music to them. Bernie was a brilliant lyricist and could make instant changes if necessary.

During the spring of '96 we were ensconced at the ranch to write and record the first album which came to be entitled *Last Stand in Open Country*. We would write in the morning and record in the afternoon. Often two songs a day. It was so easy with such great lyrics. Jim and I would go through the lyric and figure out how to put them to the right style of music. We mainly used acoustic guitars on that first record with the addition of slide guitar from yours truly. I think we recorded over twenty songs for that album and chose twelve for the final cut. Two of the songs from that record, 'This Face' and 'Last Stand in Open Country' were covered by Willie Nelson on his album, *The Great Divide*. I'm a huge fan of Willie Nelson and felt quite proud that he recorded those songs.

I picked up the phone one day at the ranch and it was Elton on the line. We chatted for a while then he asked me if I would be able to join his band for an upcoming tour. Sadly I had to decline as a new Johnny Hallyday tour was coming up. Thinking back, it could have been a great time as Elton is a lovely bloke and his guitarist Davey Johnstone is a great friend. Never mind... we finished the record and had a release party at 'The Farmers Market' in the Fairfax district of Los Angeles. The party was sponsored by Sky Vodka. Perfect! Lots of martinis and nibbles whilst the album was played. We then went on a promo tour for the album and did many radio interviews. We were all very happy with the CD and it received wonderful reviews, but it didn't really chart well. All I can say is there's no accounting for taste. Perhaps I'm biased.

We changed labels from Discovery Records to Sire Records for the second album. This time we decided to make the album slightly more rock 'n' roll than acoustic. So we invited Tad Wadhams to play bass and the wonderful Tony Brock to sit in on drums. By this time Dennis Tufano was no longer with the band. Bernie, Jim and I took to the same format of writing. Bernie gave us the lyrics and Jim and I produced the music for them. Again David Cole was on board to record and co-produce. It was another great experience and lovely to have a rhythm section with us. That CD was called *Immigrant Sons*. We worked very fast as usual and the recordings turned out really well. Tad recalled his first experience of working with us, 'I'll never forget Robin and Jim Cregan teaching me how to play an old school 50s style rock groove! I was a bit indignant at first when they told me gently that I was playing the bass groove WRONG, since, after all, I was the American in the band! They patiently dissected the beat, told me exactly what to play, Tony Brock entered with the proper drum beat (which of course he already knew how to play), Robin and Jim kicked in with the guitar figures and the whole rehearsal studio lifted into the air and flew away!'

A US tour was planned to promote the album for which Bernie put in $100,000. We called up our old friend Pete Buckland to be tour manager and we even had a proper crew to join us. We had fun, and although we didn't play huge venues, we did go to the major cities – New York, Boston San Francisco, Nashville and others. We played at 'The Roxy' on Sunset Boulevard, which was a sell out and a great show. Johnny Hallyday and most of the band were in the audience as we were about to start rehearsals for the '98 tour. In fact since 1998 we have always rehearsed in LA with Johnny.

In 1998 France won the World Cup and we were due to play three nights at Le Stade de France stadium, where in June the victorious French team defeated Brazil and lifted the trophy (I'm only writing this to keep any football fans interested). Anyway this venue, which we also played on two other later tours, holds 85,000 people. Pretty big to say the least! On that show we had a symphony orchestra and a 400 voice choir. That particular tour was called Allumer Le Feu, or in English, Light The Fire. It was a huge production with a 'B' stage in the middle of the stadium. We were doing production and sound check rehearsals and all seemed to go to plan. When it came to the first night the weather didn't look good at all and, just before we were to go on, the heavens opened up and it was decided that we had to cancel because there was no roof to cover the orchestra. Obviously the rain would have damaged their instruments irreparably. So that night was scheduled three days later. Meanwhile, our production company hastily built a roof for the orchestra in case of the same thing happening again.

We did the next two shows with glorious weather and all went well except for another hiccup. A journalist from one of the Parisian press reviewed the first show we played and accused us of playing to tape. The idiot was on the floor about seventy-five or so yards back from the stage and because of the speed of light and the difference in the speed of sound, it looked like we were out of sync with the video screens. I remember doing an interview with TF1 (one of the national television stations in France) and telling them, 'It's all absolutely live, no playback.' Johnny actually sued the paper for defamation of character (only for one Franc, just to make a point), and won the case. That journalist never came to another gig!

So it came to the night of the rescheduled show and up opened the heavens again, but even worse this time! We had the roof so the orchestra was covered and the group were all on wireless transmitters so there was no chance of electrocution. But, the rain was so heavy it dulled the strings on my guitar, so every two songs I had to change to a spare whilst my guitar tech, Lulu, put on a new set of strings and dried the soaked guitar. I must have gone through fifteen sets of strings that night. The other amazing thing about that show was that the audience all stayed through the torrential rain. It was quite special. The more we gave to them, the more they gave back to us.

Johnny was invited to play for the 2000 millennium at the Eiffel Tower in Paris. This was going to be quite something! The show was broadcast live on TF1 and on the radio as well. The stage was just in front of the tower, which was obviously closed to the public at the time.

It took days to set up as we needed twenty towers for video and sound, ten either side to go down the park in front of the tower. We went the day before the show for sound check and to make sure everything would be right. All was good. It was a free concert and so we expected quite a crowd, but we couldn't possibly guess how huge it turned out to be...

It was actually difficult to get to the venue on the day of the show due to the crowds and the traffic. And even with all the right credentials, the police made it hard for us all to get backstage. The only other time I'd seen so much security was when we played a special show for Jacques Chirac when there were more snipers on surrounding roofs than in *Call of Duty*! We had an opening act of sorts – the chorus of the girls from the Crazy Horse, a cabaret and burlesque show that's been going for years in Paris. They all looked exactly the same – topless, sporting blonde wigs and gleaming smiles. I know that half of them were 'trannies', but needless to say they were all incredibly good looking.

It was twilight as we got on the stage and I have never seen such a mass of people in my life. They seemed to go on forever. A huge sea of people chanting, 'Johnny, Johnny, Johnny.' The band was great – we played for about three hours and the music was followed by an enormous fireworks display peaking at the top of the tower. I was told there were a million plus people at that gig that night and nearly ten million watched the event on television. I read in the press the next day that a Parisian woman got into an argument with her husband, who wasn't happy that she left their flat at 3am to be able to get a good spot in front of the stage. Apparently the row turned into a fight and she ended up stabbing her husband! I don't think she ever made it to the show.

A few years later I was passing the Eiffel Tower on my way from the airport for another tour and looking at it I wondered if we would ever play there again. A couple of weeks later, our production manager Roger Abriol told me that we had been asked by Nicolas Sarkozy, the then French President, to do another gig there on Bastille Day. Johnny really is a national treasure – a journalist in one newspaper even wrote, 'We have the Louvre, the Eiffel Tower and we also have Johnny Hallyday.'

While doing one show at Le Dome (The Vélodrome) in Marseilles Johnny was performing an unplugged section. He knelt down on the floor and emulated making love to his acoustic guitar. The trouble was he got stuck down there on his knees and couldn't get up. Two of the roadies came on stage and dragged him to his feet – Johnny's hip had come out of its socket. He was manipulated by four guys offstage and he returned to the performance and, being the true professional he is, finished the concert – although he required hospitalisation afterwards!

In 1999, Jules and I decided to get married. We were actually at a party at Jim Cregan's house when we made the announcement. Bernie Taupin was there and insisted on having the wedding at his ranch where we had recorded the two Farm Dogs albums. A few weeks were spent going to and from the ranch to make arrangements and a stag night was arranged at Le Dôme restaurant (Where else?). We actually started out at a bowling alley, which was intentionally ironic as all my pals knew I hated most sports. Funnily enough I actually enjoyed the ten pin bowling! And yes… there were strippers… at the Le Dôme – not the bowling alley.

We were wed on 15ᵗʰ May 1999 and had about eighty guests. The actual wedding took place at the bottom of the hill near the pond and we were married by Tad Wadhams, Farm Dogs' bass player, who moonlights as a sort of minister, although I have to say in America anyone can get a licence online to perform marriages. Jim Cregan was my best man and Kristen Blutman was Jules' maid of honour. She and Jules had been very close friends for years. I remember messing up the vows when Tad asked me, 'Do you Robin take Jules to be your wife…?' I replied, 'Yes.' Tad said, 'I haven't finished yet.' The whole crowd cracked up, but it went smoothly after that. Both Jules' mum and dad came to the wedding even though they'd split up years previously and hadn't really talked to each other for a very long time.

Tad delivered an extraordinarily lyrical wedding speech, written specially for us by Bernie Taupin, and which I make no apology for reproducing in its entirety.

'If life is hills and valleys and we walk between them and within them, there are turns, choices and decisions each and all of us make. Some of us follow stars, some a straight path, some follow the leaders and some follow the followers but in the end it is our heart that we follow and it is our heart that eventually leads us in the right direction. A heart is not without fault, it is a compass, a barometer by which we measure our

souls. It is a magnet with a forcefield of unimaginable power. But it has in matters of the heart one simple purpose. It takes us to the source of our longing and leads us to compare lives, passion, words and sensuality. It leaves us to break down walls and bare ourselves naked; we strip down our senses and expose our vulnerability. We test each other, talk of a future, if shared as possible, and then without fear we allow ourselves to count stars, hear the waves, reflect on songs that move us and when peace glows like an ember in our eyes we discover love.

Like so many of us Robin and Julie have followed their fair share of stars, not the mortal ones I might add but those in the firmament. Neither one, I imagine, has trod a wholly straight path, detours along life's highway must have been too inviting to resist. They are, after all, an adventurous duo so following followers I can guarantee would not be an option.

They have been brought together out of a passion for living, a common bond of caring and devotion. It is easy to detect in the casual way they make loving each other look so simple.

On occasions like these we tend to turn to prophets and romantic poets for the correct words to describe the feelings of those present and more importantly the feelings of the bride and groom. Perhaps today we should leave Shakespeare and the Testaments closed. For whatever your beliefs on creation and the words that might describe it can never compare with what the eye beholds.

Robin and Julie stand together in this natural church. Two people in love under the roof of the sky and surrounded by the blanket of these hills. No mantras or clichés can compare with what nature has to teach us of humility, trust and love. It says it quietly, it whispers it on the wind. It is carried on the wings of birds and falls with the rays of the sun. It is heard in the rain and when the grass grows and when the twilight brings the moon and when the moon makes way for the dawn we witness the greatest celebration life has to offer. In this environment today the sun will set and the moon will ascend for Robin and Julie and when the dawn appears over these hills tomorrow their love will rise with it and challenge the future.'

My wedding to Jules. Visions in white... well, one of us is.

The reception was held outside under white awnings. Bernie's brother Kit is a great chef and he created some wonderful food. We decided we should have a Mexican vibe, so instead of champagne for the toast we would have tequila infused with fruit. We had lots of close friends there including Rod and dear Kiefer Sutherland. Farm Dogs played three or four songs. Kiefer came up and sang 'Knocking on Heaven's Door', and Rod came up and we did 'Sweet little Rock 'n' Roller'.

Naturally, a huge amount of tequila and wine was consumed. It was fantastic fun, with much eating and toasting to complement the drinking. Jim proposed a wonderfully touching toast, 'This will be a toast made by an Irishman to a French sounding Englishman who's marrying an Italian-American at a Californian ranch hosted by an English cowboy-lyricist and performed by a monopedic musician-minister who is not even from here... but who is? This is a great occasion for making friends, getting re-acquainted with some old ones, settling scores, and burying hatchets. Drinking, dancing, and celebrating the blessing of love. Love, without which we would not have reason to gather today.

For not only is it the force of life itself it is also so singularly the most popular topic for songwriters and... 'Ain't Love Been Good To Me?' Robin and I have been friends for twenty years or so and we are still waiting to have a row... give it time. There is obviously no rush!

And I am so honoured to be best man today. We have toured the world together in pursuit of the perfect Martini and some of them have occasionally come close. Still the search goes on. He is the kindest of men, his generosity of spirit is boundless and his quiet depth of understanding is remarkable in one so young. And this love affair with Julie is just the beginning of the really good stuff.

Julie said one day that this is a hard crowd to get to know, and she is right, we protect each other as any family does. We support one another, and as she has become beloved of us all, she is seeing that strength surrounding and nurturing her. We cannot choose our blood family but when your friends become family to you, you have the best of it all.

I propose this toast to Robin and Julie, may their love endure all seasons and inspire the sacred in us all.'

Two days later, Jules and I journeyed to Cabo San Lucas in Mexico for our honeymoon. Perfect for us! Going through Mexican customs is a stop or go experience. You wait in a queue to press a button on a stand in front of you. If a green light comes on you are fine and free to pass through, but if you get the red light you are searched. It's totally random. On another occasion we visited Mexico, and Jules decided to bring her own tortilla chips and her low calorie 'Skinny Girl Margarita'. Of course we got the red light and when they opened Jules' case they found these items. They looked at her in amazement as if she was 'loco'. Mexico is the land of chips and tequila! They let us through while falling about with laughter.

When I wasn't working with Johnny, I was involved in various projects and there was one particularly unusual job. The year was 2002 and The LA Lakers, the city's iconic basketball team, had won the NBA championship for the third year in a row. The celebration was to be held in downtown LA in front of the convention centre with an estimated crowd of about 300,000 people. At that time, their adopted song was Queen's 'We Will Rock You' and I was asked to play Brian May's solo guitar part which comes in the middle of the song. I had to record the drums and use a digital SMPTE (the Society of Motion Picture and Television Engineers) time code for cueing the lights and fireworks. But I performed the guitar part! A large stage was erected with sound and lighting towers, plus a huge riser behind the stage that would lift the team as I was close to finishing the music. I must say I felt a little alone and vulnerable in front of the crowd but it went off without a hitch. The game and the song was on all the local TV networks that night and I received so many calls asking if that was me. Well, yes it was!

Sometime in April or May 2004, Jules, Rod and his wife Penny and I were having dinner when Rod told me that guitarist Jeff Golub would not be on the US/Canadian tour and after a few minutes of chat, it was agreed that I would fill in for Jeff. So I was to be treading the boards again with my old cohort. Before the tour began, Jules and I were invited to go on a holiday with Rod, Penny and two other couples. He had a chartered a motor yacht and we were to cruise round the Mediterranean for ten days. Now, I've done this kind of trip before with Johnny and I knew to expect a fantastic time! The only caveat for me was that I had to leave the boat about three days before the end of the trip as I had to be back in LA to start rehearsals for the tour, though

Jules would stay on. The boat was called 'Braveheart' and was 185 feet long with more crew than guests!

Jules and I flew via Paris because I had a meeting there and then we travelled to Naples to board the boat. The crew were amazing. One of the girls took our luggage to our state room and unpacked for us, placing everything in order in the drawers and making us feel very comfortable. Nothing was too much to ask of them. They were so helpful in every way. The great thing about that type of holiday is that we would stop in Capri, have lunch on the boat, dinner on the island, go back for a nightcap on the boat, sleep and during the night the boat would travel to next destination. It's truly a fabulous holiday.

When it was time for me to leave everyone and fly back to LA for the rehearsals, Rod was very laid back and suggested I stay on board for the duration of the cruise but I knew I had to leave. I didn't want to let the band down – apart from that I knew I would never hear the end of it from them! I left the yacht when we got to Corsica and took the plane to Paris and then on to LA. As soon as I landed I was taken to 3rd Encore, a rehearsal studio in north Hollywood and got straight into working. I felt completely exhausted but I knew the band really well so I was comfortable with them, kind of like putting on a comfortable suit you haven't worn for ages. After a week or so we went to Orlando in Florida for three days of production rehearsals where the first show was to take place.

I think it went well… at least I don't remember it going badly. On stage, Rod introduced me by saying, 'This is Robin Le Mesurier, he comes from a theatrical background – his brother's a curtain.' Or, 'This is Robin Le Mesurier, he was in the group three hundred years ago.' It's funny, often the first show of a tour goes well and the second night can be a disaster. Then it'll smooth out and be fine for the rest. But, having said that, there was one time my guitar tech handed me a guitar with the wrong tuning! And Don Kirkpatrick (the other guitarist) and I were doing the intro to 'Tonight's the Night' which was really awful. Of course he apologised to me profusely but you can't 'unring a bell'.

The shows were in two parts. During the first half, which lasted about an hour, we performed the regular Rod songs. During the intermission, behind closed curtains, our amazing crew, in about twelve minutes, turned the stage into a 'forties' band stand, the stage itself being transformed from stark white into a 1940s black Art Deco design. We changed into 'black tie' for the second half of the show, the 'Great American Song Book' and did about forty minutes of classic American songs such as 'As Time Goes By', 'I've Got You Under My Skin', and more from Rod's albums of those great songs he covered. The standards were actually quite difficult to play for those uninitiated with them. We actually had to read music and the only one I knew by heart was 'Sunny Side of the Street'. Some of those classic numbers contain some very unusual chords – a bit different to twelve bar blues! After the 'songbook' section, we returned to Rod's roots and finished the set with 'Maggie May', 'You Wear it Well', 'Do you Think I'm Sexy?' and 'Stay with Me' etc. which took up another twenty-five minutes or so. So, the audience got a whole range of Rod's music history.

One of most treasured memories is playing the last show of the tour, at the Hollywood Bowl, at the end of August 2004. It was a fantastic concert and the band was joined by ex Faces Ronnie Wood and Ian Mclagan. Ruby, Rod's daughter, sang a couple of numbers – I think one of them was 'Brass in Pocket', The Pretender's hit. The encore was the Faces song, 'Ooh La La'.

I did receive a worried phone call from Johnny, who happened to be in Orlando asking me that now I was back playing with Rod, was I leaving his band? 'No chance,' I told him. 'You can't get rid of me that easily.' And I was soon back with Johnny's band.

Geoff Dugmore is a great mate and one of the best drummers in the business. He wrote these very kind words about me in a book a few years ago, 'It's not often in life you find a friend who embodies everything, the most wonderful musicianship… a true gentleman and a one of a kind. Just check out the intro to "Dans La Rue" from the JH Flashback tour. That's what I'm talking about – a man that puts a guitar round his neck and makes it swing.'

Now you can see why he's one of my closest friends! Born in Glasgow, Geoff formed a band called Motion Pictures with a couple of friends and moved to London at the age of seventeen. The band changed their name to The Europeans in early 1981 and they recorded three albums with A&M. Joan Armatrading heard him play and immediately wanted him to record with her. Since then Geoff has been in constant demand for live gigs and session recordings. He's actually been involved in the recordings of fifty number one hits! He tells a funny story about Tina Turner during one of these sessions. Recording the *Foreign Affair* album in London in 1988, Tina arrived and made straight for Geoff and her opening line was, 'Feel my thighs.' Geoff didn't quite know what to do or what might happen if he didn't react, but did as I was told and said, 'Yeah, your thighs feel great.' Tina appreciated his remark and told him that she had been working out in the gym. That was Geoff's introduction to Tina Turner.

Geoff had recorded a few albums with Johnny and in 2006 was asked to tour with the band. He rang me to ask what I thought, what it would be like and what to expect being on the road with such an icon. I think he was talking about 'the singer' – not me! Anyway, I said it would be great. I was delighted. I had known Geoff from years ago when we used to knock around the Marquee and Browns in the 1970s but we had never worked together. His audition with Johnny was a dinner at The Ivy having to prove how much he could drink. He passed with flying colours.

We hit it off at the first rehearsal and Geoff later told me, 'It was like finding a brother I never knew I had.' I felt the same way. He also told me that he was little nervous – it's always difficult finding your feet in a new band especially working with someone so famous as Johnny, but he also told me that I helped him settle into the band and became a sort of mentor. In fact he's always nagging me to pass on my blues style, which we describe as 'Rucka Rucka', to the next generation of younger guitarists. 'Rucka Rucka' was originally invented by Chuck Berry. Billy Peek, from Rod's band, played with Chuck and learned the technique from the rock 'n' roll legend himself. The method is that when you strike the guitar strings with your right hand, you slightly dampen the strings with your left hand to stop the strings vibrating. That's what they call 'Rucka Rucka'.

I've always been a stickler for punctuality – if there is a lobby call for 10am, I'll always be there by 9.40 am – even though I only have to make my way from my hotel room downstairs. I think it's rude to keep people waiting – a sort of selfish trait that your time is more important than theirs. Geoff always reckons if he sees me on my way anywhere, he has about twenty minutes to get ready...

Geoff and I have shared a dressing room from the very first concert and called it 'The Knob and Bollocks'. We refer to each other by nicknames we've given ourselves. Posh barmaids, in fact... I'm 'Lavinia' and Geoff is 'Dolores'. We fly the Saltire, the flag of Scotland and the Union Jack or Flag of St George – and then other band members have since added their flags – we have a Polish harmonica player, Greg Zlap, and the stars and stripes for a couple of Americans on board and the Tricolor of course. In fact everyone gravitates to our dressing room before the off.

I'll have vodka, but Geoff doesn't imbibe any alcohol before the show. We also have a pre-gig play list starting with 'Pool Hall Richard' by the Faces and once guitar solo begins we both call out. 'And they're off'. Another track results in us asking each other, 'Does my bum look big in this?' The playlist lasts an hour and includes 'Rock and Roll' (Led Zeppelin), 'Back In Black' (ACDC), 'When I Get Drunk' (Mike Henderson And The Bluebloods), 'Rough Justice' (The Rolling Stones), 'Sweet Little Rock 'n' Roller', and 'Let It Rock' (Chuck Berry), 'Tush' (ZZ Top).

Geoff sprays me three times with whatever cologne he happens to be using at the time and we end with 'Up yer bum, dear!' The traditions are exactly the same as when we started in the band together ten years ago and have passed from a bit of fun into serious rituals – we have to go through them for fear of something going wrong if we don't follow them in order! No, we're not paranoid... just a little daft I suppose.

During the song 'Gabrielle' Geoff goads me into a bit of showmanship and I perform a few Peter Townshend type 'windmills'. I once dropped my pick and had to go through the routine without it – I shredded my fingers quite badly. You see it's quite dangerous being a rock 'n' roll guitarist.

Johnny sees everything and hears everything – he appreciates band members not only for their musicianship but also for their showmanship. And he really wants the band to go that extra mile in terms of their commitment. He never sings much in rehearsals, but when he comes on stage he gives it absolutely everything. Quite often before a gig he'll say to me, 'Robin, I'm tired,' but as soon as he steps on the stage he's a new man. I'm sure that's the actor in him. And he's he's a very good actor, having made many films. He won 'Best Actor' award at The Venice Film

The 'three sweetie darlings' as we call ourselves!
On tour with Geoff Dugmore (drums, centre) Alain Lanty (keyboards, left) and moi.

Festival for *L'homme du Train* (Man on the train). Not only does he possess incredible charisma, but his voice is unique. I'll never forget the first time I heard him in the studio when we recorded 'Quelque Chose de Tennessee', an elegiac song about Tennessee Williams which had already been a huge hit of his and is a staple on every show we do. Johnny was in the vocal booth when we played the intro and when he came in, his voice just blew me away! And still does on every show we do.

At the live shows, and wherever we are, the first two or three rows are often occupied by the same audience members. They must save up and take holidays to come to every night of the tour. It's incredibly humbling – the fans become part of the show and even the performance, comparing notes on every song in every gig. They even wish each other 'good luck' before the show. We are all grateful for such devotion – we'd be out of work without them. And now I've noticed, we have a new set of fans, from a younger generation and despite their youth they all know the lyrics and join in, which Johnny loves; 'It's good when the audience sing along – I don't have to work so hard.' Ha!

One of my staunchest fans is Cathy Vivier. We had already played twenty-two nights at The Palais de Sports on the 2006 Flashback Tour, where I might add as soon as we finished the shows, many of the crowd would leave the arena only to camp outside to be the first to get in the next day! Talk about being hardcore fans. Later on we were to play again at Bercy arena in Paris for another few nights, and our wonderful tour manager at that time, Bruno Batlo, delivered me a letter from a fan. Basically it read, 'I'd like to introduce myself to you. I first saw you in 1998 when my dad took me to a Johnny Hallyday concert and had complete admiration for you.' She then went on to ask if she could create a website for me. At first I thought she might be one of those crazily obsessive fans that inhabit the music world. But I was completely wrong. We eventually met and she turned out to be very sweet and totally genuine. And to my amazement, she bought the domain name robinlemesurier.com (which I never thought of doing myself), and built a really good site, with history, media content, photographs, contact information, which to this day has helped people getting in touch with me, the guitars I use, amps etc. etc. She still runs the site and we have become very good friends. She and her husband Fred even came to Scotland to attend two shows I played later with the band called Apart

From Rod. Loyalty or what? As the Chuck Berry song goes, '"C'est la vie" say the old folks, it goes to show you never can tell'. Cathy also produced a couple of books about me with fabulous photographs and lovely quotes, which I treasure. I always see her and her husband Fred when I can when I'm in France. It's always a pleasure to see her. She really is a great girl.

The Tour 66 was billed as Johnny's last major tour (it wasn't of course) and named after the famous iconic Route 66 that traverses the USA and a symbol of Johnny's love of American rock music. It was also a nod in the direction of Johnny's age – he was sixty-six in 2009, the year of the tour. The sets were incredible; the stage was dominated by an enormous mythical bird, with wings outstretched to an enormous span. There was a huge Route 66 shield emblem and four robots moved video screens during the show. At the Stade de France performance, about sixty Harley Davisons were driven across the stage. The Health and Safety officials must have had heart attacks.

The tour continued through to November and the following month I was supposed to have dinner with Johnny in LA, but I hadn't heard back from him, which was unusual. I spoke to his wife, Laeticia who told me that the back operation Johnny underwent in France had been botched (he had fallen on his yacht near Monaco during the summer); he had been taken ill and admitted to hospital (Johnny and Laeticia later sued the French surgeon). I went to see him and he told me that he had been in hospital for a night when in fact he had been placed into a medically-induced coma for nearly a week. Johnny's hospitalisation had gone almost unnoticed in the US, where he was described as the 'French Elvis' but once news leaked out the French press, including journalists from newspapers and *Oui* and *Paris Match* magazines, were camped out outside the Cedars-Sinai hospital.

Johnny's hospitalisation even attracted the attention of French President Nicolas Sarkozy, who described Johnny as 'greatly loved… have confidence in him… he's tough.' Valerie Cantie, a journalist who reported on the story for Radio France stated, 'I covered Michael Jackson's death and I'm more exhausted with Johnny Hallyday.' We were supposed to be resuming our Tour 66 after Christmas but we had to cancel because of Johnny's health. Thank goodness Johnny lived to tour another day.

FOOL FOR THE BLUES
Music by Robin Le Mesurier – lyrics by Paul Rafferty

Don't say you love me babe,
I know you'd be lying
I can see it in your smile
It's like a drug now
You're addicted to them blues
Always getting high
Oh! But the rain it falls
From the way I feel, the way I feel

Empty souls and empty hearts
We don't choose, I'm still a
Fool the blues.

Oh those bitter words
How they hurt me baby
Do someone hurt you bad?
All this pain
We have inside all of us
From the love we never had
Oh! And the rain still falls
But I know baby through it all
Oh! They say time will heal
But I know from the way I feel, the way I feel

Empty souls and empty hearts we don't choose
I'm still a fool the blues
Empty souls and empty hearts we don't choose
I'm still a fool the blues

9

REHAB

In the summer of 2011 I was drinking a bottle of vodka a night – I started imbibing every evening at 6pm when I fed the dogs – our two little white Jack Russells, Harry and Maude. Yes, named from the movie *Harold and Maude*. Anyway, it had become a habit and, although loathe to admit it, I was becoming too dependent on alcohol. Dad had died from the results of excess drinking although, of course, I didn't see mine as serious, but deep down I suppose I knew something needed to change. And then as has often been the way in my 'charmed life' an opportunity arose which was perfect timing. Timing is often everything.

My agent in LA, Sherri Thomas called me one Friday afternoon and asked me if I would like to go to Rehab. Rehab? What immediately came to mind was a story about Ronnie Wood going to rehab and Keith Richards sending him a bouquet of flowers with a note attached which read, 'Rehab is for quitters'. Never checked with Ronnie to see if it was true, but coming from Keith it's funny. There was a slight twist to this suggestion because *Rehab* was the title of a reality English television show, in which a group of celebrities with alcohol or drug or other addictions would enter a rehabilitation centre in Malibu and be filmed for the duration of their stay.

Sherri wasn't aware of my excessive drinking problem and so this was what you might call some serious synchronicity. I was pretty reluctant but realised a rest and the $30,000 fee would do me good! I asked her who else was going to be involved and when I was told that

Victoria Sellers (Britt Ekland and Peter Sellers' daughter), who had a drug problem and Les McKeown (The Bay City Rollers), a self confessed alcoholic, were coming along – both of whom were old friends and so I decided I'd go for it.

I was contacted by a representative of Endemol, the production company, who said I would need to be interviewed by a psychologist to see if I was 'fit' enough not only to cope with the confines of a residential institution, but also the stress and pressure of being able to talk publicly about my drinking and personal stuff whilst being filmed and then the whole thing being broadcast on national television. Well, the psychologist and Endemol seemed to think I was up to it – I suppose if I could survive a Rod Stewart tour, I could cope with most things.

I returned home to Los Angeles after the interviews and was told that I would be picked up on Sunday night and taken to the rehabilitation centre where I would spend a fortnight in various forms of therapy. The institution was called *Passages* and nestled up above the Pacific Coast Highway in the lush hills of Malibu.

When the crew came to pick me up I was encouraged… no, pushed… to drink a couple of very large vodka martinis whilst they were shooting and interviewing me in my kitchen. I later discovered they used the same modus operandi for all the other British contributors everyone flying from the UK to LA. I suppose they thought that if the viewers saw us all arriving drunk and shaky, it would make better television viewing.

Let me tell you a little bit about the very plush *Passages*, which has been jokingly described as 'The Heaven's Gate of Rehabs'. The place was founded in 2001 by Chris Prentiss, a Los Angeles businessman, whose son Pax had become addicted to heroin, cocaine and alcohol. Pax had been in various rehab programmes without success and so Chris started his own. Treatment at *Passages* includes individual and family therapists, life coaches, nutritionists, hypnotherapists, masseuses and acupuncturists. I think that's everyone…

The food was prepared by a top chef and was, of course, extremely nutritious, and attempted to cater to each resident's favourite grub. I don't actually remember a Sunday roast though. We were subjected to an introduction by Chris Prentiss in which he said that *Passages* wasn't the usual rehab institution – instead it was a 'Spiritual Transformation

Centre'. His favourite word was 'perfect', and even if something bad had happened in the past it could still be termed 'perfect' because it... happened. A few of us found it difficult to get our heads around that I must say. In fact it seemed complete gobbledygook but there you are. We were all ensconced in our new home for two weeks and had to get on with it.

Set in ten acres, the main building with marble hallways and elegant antique furniture was enhanced by a koi pond and a state of the art gym. The residential accommodation was actually stunning – a beautiful little gated community with Mediterranean style villas each having four or five bedrooms in each building. I think there were four houses plus the main meeting and dining room, offices, nurses' station and reception.

Luckily, they put me in the pool house which was fine so I didn't have to share a room with anyone. And the view over the Pacific Ocean was gorgeous. The rest of the group for the series were already there when I arrived. There were lots of hugs and greetings from my friendly inmates, enquiring how each was doing. The first thing I had to do was pee in order to test the alcohol level in my blood stream. I reckon if I had driven there and been stopped by the police I would have been thrown right in the clink! Then there was some paperwork to complete and a short introduction explaining what form the rehab would take over the next two weeks.

The first evening we just sat around and chatted about why we were there and about our various addictions. *Passages* is nothing like Alcoholics Anonymous with a twelve step program. They treat addiction as a behavioural problem rather than an illness and the rationale is that whatever one's addiction is, it can be treated by the staff, who would work with everyone very differently. For example, one of my cohorts was Alicia Douvall who was addicted to plastic surgery! Not drink or drugs. She had already had quite a number of procedures and, as far as I know, still hasn't stopped – despite her time in *Passages*. I got on with her very well. She had a great sense of humour and I enjoyed her company and she has since become a veteran of reality TV shows.

In fact I got on with everyone on our sojourn. There was Cassie Sumner, a model and actress with bulimia (now with two children and happily married to Jose Fonte, a Portuguese international footballer) and the singer Rowetta, once with The Happy Mondays, who was battling alcoholism. There was one American guy in our group – who didn't seem to have an addiction or need to be there at all. Sean Kanan – a soap actor with a dependency on pain killers. There were, of course, other residents at *Passages*, but we never really mixed other than at meal times.

A day or so after we got there, we all had to see the resident doctor for all sorts of blood tests and physical examinations. Of course, the cameras followed us most of the time, though it wasn't like *Big Brother*, which has cameras everywhere, capturing everything that goes on. Anyway the doctor asked me what my personal addiction was and I replied somewhat casually, 'Drinking too much.' I suppose it was understandable that she didn't seem particularly surprised and nonchalantly replied, 'OK. Let's do some tests.' I was there for what seemed to be an eternity having blood drawn while being questioned about drinking habits, my alcohol intake and how I felt the alcohol was affecting me.

Two days later, I went to see her again to receive the test results. I must admit I was a little worried as to what she would tell me. The camera crew were there with us as she studied the forms. She stared at the papers in front of her and, shaking her head in a bewildered fashion, looked at me and said, 'I can't believe what I'm seeing.' My heart sank. I thought I was in trouble and nervously muttered, 'What can't you believe?' She told me that my blood levels looked completely normal. And my liver, kidneys and cholesterol all appeared to be perfectly normal. She smiled at me, 'You must have great genes.' You can imagine how I felt hearing those words. I was greatly relieved and not a little surprised. She then confided in me and said that everyone in my group that came from the UK had high amounts of mercury and arsenic in their systems! I was too shocked to ask why, but just got out the room as quickly as I could.

The time I spent at *Passages* consisted of about 75% one on one with a counsellor and 25% in group therapy. I have to say that group therapy really wasn't my scene. The idea of baring my soul in public was something of an anathema. The girls were much more able to share their feelings and fears and became very emotional. Naturally, the individual therapy sessions confidential and were never discussed.

In one of my filmed interviews I attempted to justify my drinking. 'I know that my mum and dad used to smoke pot when I was growing up and a lot of people did. The entertainment industry and drugs go hand in hand. The Rod Stewart group were very much party animals and it would take about three songs into the show that I sweated out all the previous night's alcohol. At home I drink vodka. Not a bottle a night but it's still way too much. Maybe two thirds or three quarters of a bottle but not a full bottle.' Of course it was true about my drinking when on the road with Rod, but even at home, I was drinking at least a bottle of vodka a night, but because I was in good health, I thought I was getting away with it.

Nearly all my personal sessions were directed to my childhood and upbringing. It was quite painful at times and always very emotional. I was brought to tears a number of times talking about Mum and Dad, their relationship and how I dealt with it at the time. It's funny, but these sessions seemed to affect me more than their actual divorce when I was a child. I suppose we accept things much more readily when children and it's only in retrospect when we're more analytical that formative experiences take on more meaning. Perhaps in those days I saw the way my dad was dealing with the split with Mum and all the upheaval and I followed his cue – something I have done a number of times over the years.

There was one therapist I saw every day, her name was Athena Lennon (no relation to John) and on one occasion she said, 'You look so familiar to me,' to which I replied, 'And you to me.' She looked at me quizzically, 'I know you're in the music business,' she continued, 'do you know an agent called Rod Mcsween?' I did. He was Rod Stewart's agent some time ago and consequently we spent that entire hour reminiscing and talking about mutual friends. Not quite an intense therapy session… but much more fun.

A couple of weeks after I left *Passages*, Jules and I went to Palm Springs, where we were going to stay with friends. I picked up some wine from a supermarket and then ran into Athena, clutching two bottles of champagne and some ice cream. Of course we stopped and chatted for a short time, but she didn't say anything about the wine I was carrying. I don't think she even cared about what I was getting up to. But, it made me feel as if I was caught with my hand in the cookie jar.

I had one session with a hypnotherapist, Mary Lou Kenworthy. She put me in what she described was a 'dream like trance' but it felt more like I was in limbo between dreaming and knowing where I was and what I was doing. I told Mary that I had seen saw a lost seven-year-old child, which was true. I was told it was 'very healing' and 'wonderful for you.' I suppose it was healing to a certain extent, although not quite so sure about wonderful it was. But it did give me courage and made me feel good about myself.

Some of the sessions dealt with trust issues and a couple were outdoors; one was canoeing in Pacific Ocean with a partner. I picked Victoria as my partner as I knew her the best and we actually did fine. I can't remember who, but a couple of them capsized and lived to tell the tale. Another test was very frightening. Victoria and I had to climb a pole which was attached by a cable to another pole about fifty yards away. There were then a series of posts placed further and further apart and we had to try and get from one post to the other by holding hands and slowly walking on the cables to the opposite pole. We had harnesses attached to us, but it was still pretty scary.

I think we got about half way across, but then lost the battle and fell to the ground, albeit gently, mind you, as we had safety ropes. The other personal test for us all was to climb a post which was about fifty feet high with a trapeze bar ten feet or so hanging in front at the top of the pole. Now, I can't stand heights, and found it very difficult standing on top of it as it was only one foot in diameter! Eventually, with encouragement from the guys down below, I took a deep breath feeling as if my heart was about to burst out of my chest and jumped into thin air. God only knows how I managed to grab the trapeze bar but thankfully I did and slowly descended to Mother Earth. I was trembling and very breathless. Under no circumstances will I ever do that again. I saw the whole thing on a DVD when I was sent 'my' episode, and watching it I thought I must have been out of my mind to take that on that challenge.

At that time Jules and I were going through a bit of a sticky period in our relationship. I have to say this was mostly my fault because of my being so insular and not talking about my feelings. I have to admit I am still guilty of this and have to be nudged sometimes to open up.

Somewhat ironic really because that's exactly what I'm doing now. Mum and Dad were very much like this and I think it was either in the genes or learned behaviour.

Jules came to visit me a couple of times when I was at *Passages* and we had a couple of sessions together. When I saw the DVD, there was one scene that was shot outside in the beautiful grounds. Jules and I each had a chair and the therapist was sitting in front of us. Watching it later, I couldn't help but see the body language between Jules and me. We were both leaning away from each other. It was so obvious something wasn't right.

Jules was asked about my drinking and she admitted that, 'I asked him hypothetically, what would you choose… me or the drinking? He had to think about it and couldn't even answer the question. I'd rather he stopped drinking because I feel it's affecting his work, his future and I think that drinking just keeps him in that zone that whatever it's easy to numb himself. At this point I have one foot in the door and one foot out of the door and kind of moving on and see us not staying together.' She had clearly felt estranged from our marriage, but at the end of the session, we ended up holding hands and I felt that we had somehow come back together. It was very hard and I was sad to hear how it was affecting her. I didn't mean to make it so difficult for her. But I was happy that she had come to visit and I'm sure it helped our reconciliation.

Apart from my own inclination to avoid conflict at any cost, I suppose I was partly prevented from opening up by what I perceived as the situation or plight of my fellow 'cast members'. It seemed to me, the others in my group had far worse and even life threatening problems. So I kind of felt I wasn't in such a bad state. Every night we were given a sleeping pill which I found essential – especially during the first week as I had always used alcohol to help me sleep at night. We weren't allowed to take the medication until we went to bed, just in case it was used as a substitute during the day. This really pissed me off – not only because I liked to stay up late, but more importantly we clearly weren't trusted. And the other thing that annoyed me was, every night the 'night nurse', some bloke, whose name I never knew, would come to the pool house and check on me. Making sure I was there and asleep. I was never asleep, but pretended to be.

But, there was plenty of free time as well. There was one 'open mic' night when I played guitar and we sang songs. The weather was beautiful of course and we could sunbathe. Alicia was ticked off for showing off too much skin, which wasn't allowed for fear of driving the male residents wild with desire. We listened to listen to music and in the evening we would play Scrabble or Monopoly. The atmosphere was very convivial as we all got on very well and we would chat naturally and happily with each other. There was very little tension and no flare ups in the group. It certainly helped me that Victoria and Les were there. Some of us even considered writing a situation comedy based in a similar fictitious institution. It never happened.

After a week we were allowed to venture out to buy things we needed from the local market – mostly cigarettes in my case. We always had a chaperone with us, and had blood tests when we returned from the outings, just to make sure we hadn't fallen off the wagon as it were. I did buy a telescope on one shopping expedition so that I could look at the night sky. I thought about buying a map of the stars, but figured I'd most likely be sold a map of Beverly Hills! I was quite happy to relax and stargaze, which I found very calming. It was so clear we could see the island of Catalina, situated south-west of Los Angeles.

So the two weeks went by, but they seemed like an eternity. And then it was time for the UK guests to leave. Surprisingly, I was given the opportunity to stay for another fortnight – perhaps they thought I was more addicted that I realised – but what was more surprising was that I actually agreed to this extension.

Jules wanted me back, which was great, but I felt I could still benefit from the therapy. She told me, 'I don't want to be selfish but I really want you to be home with me because I want us to be together and work together.' So initially I said I would come home as I genuinely thought I was ready. But I was persuaded by my therapist, who told me I could benefit from further rehab and told me to be 'a bit more selfish'. So I gave it some more thought; I had gone two weeks without alcohol and wanted to prove to myself that I could continue sober. I'm here now, why not give it a little more time? It could actually benefit both of us. I told Jules of my decision and she was immediately incredibly supportive.

So I stayed another week. I went through the same routine most days: breakfast, three sessions, lunch, another three sessions, outings, free time, dinner and back to my beautiful view and then going online (we were allowed internet access) to see what was happening in the world as I felt a little out of touch. I gave a final interview to camera just before I departed *Passages*, 'I'm basically the same person I was when I came in here, just I have a clearer mind, I feel that blinkers have been taken off. I've learnt to dig into myself. I've learnt that for me there is more to me than I thought there was. It's been hugely beneficial, I'm really glad I stayed here but right now, it's time for me to go. I really want to be home now. It's been quite a journey and I just hope I can stay on the righteous path. I feel like I'm really ready to be home and to get on with life and start over. I don't think I'll drink again. I've had enough.'

I meant it at the time. I knew I had been drinking too much and it was time for a change of lifestyle. Although, my main counsellor told me, 'I know you well enough now, and it's ok if you have the occasional drink,' which I have to say I was very surprised to hear. And I was true to my word for a while. It must have been about a year or so later when I started drinking again but not to the extent I had been before. One of the benefits of my not drinking was I could drive with no worries about being stopped by the police and being charged with Driving Under the Influence ('DUI'). Now, if Jules and I go to a dinner party or some function where I know I'll have a drink, we'll always take an Uber or someone will drive us. I would never drink and drive again. God knows I used to in the past and could have killed myself... or someone else.

There were times when I really didn't want to be at *Passages* and other times when I was quite happy to experience the various therapies. I was amazed I actually managed to stay the course and in fact benefited from the therapy. I didn't have a drink for a long time after the show, but did inevitably return to my early evening tipple. In retrospect, Sherri's telephone call may not actually have saved my life, but it may well have saved my marriage.

However, after an extra fortnight at the institution, I was eager to get home. On my last night there, a very well dressed and clearly affluent guy came into my 'private' sanctuary (the pool house) and said, 'Hello, what's your D.O.C?' For a second or so I was confused, but replied, 'What the fuck are you talking about?' He continued, 'Drug of choice;

heroin, crack cocaine, meth, prescription drugs.' He must have been a seasoned user. I looked at him I'm sure with disdain and replied, 'None of the above – just vodka.' I went outside to smoke and thought with great happiness and anticipation about going home the next day. When I woke up in the morning I immediately began to pack my suitcase and prepared myself to sign the discharge papers and whatnot. It seemed for a moment like I was finishing a prison sentence.

A day or so before I was due to leave, I talked to Chris Prentiss and suggested that they should have music therapy as part of the therapeutic curriculum. He thought it was a great idea, so with my contacts with Fender, Line 6 manufacturers and a few other people, I managed to get everything I needed to set up a studio in one of the empty rooms. All they had to buy was an Apple computer as I could supply everything else. I suggested I could come to teach and make some recordings two or three times a week. It all looked like it was going to happen. A week or so later I set up the little studio, connected everything all together and was ready to roll.

I returned the next day and, to my horror, the computer had disappeared. Stolen! I went to the main office, told them what had happened, to which I really got a blank stare and was told that the computer hadn't been stolen – they had, in fact, changed their mind about 'music therapy'. I lost all respect with them then, as I feel music is a universal language and can be so helpful to people with problems. Oh well... I thought it was a good idea at the time. It's funny how some people can be so short sighted.

Since my stay at *Passages*, there have been complaints about the institution flouting local laws by buying up private residences and adding to the burgeoning facilities. Local Malibu residents have grumbled about the increasing numbers of people being treated there, thus increasing the traffic and the presence of large numbers of paparazzi hoping to snap a celebrity in trouble. Not to mention the sighting of an occasional disorientated patient wandering around the streets in a daze. Wouldn't be surprised if that isn't the guy trying to find his D.O.C...

10

RESTER VIVANT

In over four decades that I have been working in the music business, I have been lucky enough to have been involved in a number of diverse and interesting projects. Sherri Thomas found me television and film work that suited my character, i.e. the typecast rock 'n' roll look. Ha! I've done a few things, and one of my favourites was a television show with Brooke Shields and Eric Idle. Brooke had a series called *Suddenly Susan* in which Eric Idle appeared regularly and I was in one episode, entitled *The Bird in the Wall*, which was broadcast in June 2000. That was fun. The story was about Eric's character being a one hit wonder in England in the past with a song called 'The Sausage Shop Girl'. It was great to see Brooke again as we knew each other when she was my old friend Julian Lennon's girlfriend for a while. I got Tony Brock and Tad Wadhams from Farm Dogs to put a fictitious backing group together for Eric's band called 'The Maxtones'.

I had a few lines which I changed as the writers were a little unsure about the English language in the sixties. I remember one of the lines of 'The Sausage Shop Girl' was, 'she likes to mash and I like to banger'. I never thought that would get past the censors! There were about four days of rehearsals and a day of shooting at Warner Bros. in Studio City just over the hill in the San Fernando Valley. During the rehearsals for the show Eric and I spent a lot of time talking about Dad and he was determined to rack my brain for memories about him. We actually became quite friendly at that time. And later on I had an idea about

176

doing an album of rock 'n' roll covers like 'Sweet Little Rock 'n' Roller', 'Little Queenie', 'Honky Tonk Women' and the like but with a Noel Coward voice singing/talking the lyrics. Sadly he told me he had too much on his plate. But, I still want to make a go of it at some point in the future. Try and imagine Noel Coward's voice warbling, 'There she is again standing over by the record machine, she's too cute to be a minute over seventeen.'

Another unusual venture I became involved in was writing the soundtrack for a feature film, *Inside the Goldmine*, which was released in 1994. It was co-written, directed and starred Josh Evans, the son of Robert Evans and Ali MacGraw of *Love Story* fame, and who had appeared in *Born on the Fourth of July* with Tom Cruise. Influenced by the early films of John Cassavetes, the film featured a murder investigation involving a Hollywood producer.

That was a big learning curve. Josh Evans lived across the street from me and when he told me about the movie he was making, I immediately asked him, 'Do you need music?' A bit cheeky, perhaps, but he said he did and I said I would love to be involved. My work started after the movie was shot because music is *always* the last element in a film. Josh used to come over nearly every day and show me the scenes he wanted scoring. I composed the music using guitars and keyboards and recorded in the studio in my apartment. We would work together for hours every day and I learned something very important about writing for film. Basically, don't introduce music whenever you feel it's needed. Sometimes a scene needs suitable music to add tension, drama or excitement, but sometimes a scene needs nothing at all and the soundtrack can detract from the action.

Some years later I was having dinner with Faye Dunaway and Johnny Hallyday at Lorada and we were talking about the importance of a film's score. Believe it or not when Faye first saw the rough cut for *Chinatown* she hated it and it was only when Jerry Goldsmith added the score that she loved the movie. It was only twenty-five minutes of music, but it established the personality of each character by his use of instrumentation and avant-garde orchestration. Mind you this was a classic soundtrack from a legend in film music, who had turned his hand at every sort of movie genre and whose oeuvre included *The Omen, Gremlins, Logan's Run* and five *Star Trek* films – so I'm not comparing myself to him.

I've been involved in another movie score, but much more recently. I ran into an old friend, Nick Mead, who told me he was making a documentary entitled, *The Last American Outlaw* about a Hell's Angel called George Christie, from the Ventura Chapter (Ventura is about an hour and a half drive north from LA). George had retired from being an 'Angel' for some time but the US Government had been after him for years trying to get him on one bogus charge or another. The Inland Revenue Service wanted him for tax evasion, accusing him of evading hundreds of thousands of dollars. When an audit of his accounts was completed, he was found to owe just $85 in taxes. The Service attempted to pin other things on him but never could. They wanted him to 'snitch' on other members of the chapter and were angry that he hadn't helped them. It's obviously an unwritten rule never to do that. Anyway, I gave Nick a few tracks from my solo album, *Picture Palace*. Nick got a deal with a cable company in LA for the movie and we're hoping for a release. Fingers crossed.

My album, *Picture Palace*, was released in Japan in 1997and came from a meeting with Kaz Utsunomia, a friend at Chrysalis Records. I told him about an idea I had for a solo album based on classic American songs, notably some tunes from *West Side Story*. So the next day I went into my studio and started working on 'There's A Place For Us' and 'Maria'. I decided to blend them into a medley which turned out to be about seven minutes long. I think I started on those two because *West Side Story* was the first musical I went to when I was a child. Mum took me to see it, and the music just stuck with me.

Then I started on an instrumental version of 'Someone To Watch Over Me'. I later wrote and recorded nine other tunes. I got Tad to play bass guitar on a couple of tracks and Steven Stern and Darby Orr to help me with strings and keys. The album did ok, but wasn't a huge success and I would love to get it released here in the USA at some point. If you want a listen, it can be found on my website www.robinlemesurier.com (sorry, more product placement). Oh... I named the album Picture Palace as homage to my grandmother Mary as that's what she used to call the cinema. Fitting really as the music has a cinematic quality to it.

I've also been involved with an organisation known as the *League of Rock,* a sort of *School of Rock* but for executives in which music is the focal point for team building. The logline explains everything, 'Get your team truly connected by combining the universal language of music with the excitement of Rock 'n' Roll!' Work colleagues form rock bands and the organisation provides the instruments, rehearsal space, studio and professional producers, writers and musicians to provide expertise, guidance and help. There is also a concert where the participants get to showcase their talents. I was hired for one of these courses in Toronto in 2007 and met up with Jim McCarty who I hadn't seen for years and we performed 'Little Queenie'. *League of Rock* is a great idea and works well for all those involved, giving music fans a chance to work with professionals.

I think it was early 2008 when Chris Kimsey called me and asked if I would come over to England to record an album for a Russian artist, singer/songwriter/guitarist called Sergei Voronov (aka Voronoff) which he was producing. Once I'd established it wasn't the figure skater with the same name, I told him I would be happy to make the trip and the fact that Geoff Dugmore would be playing drums on the sessions made it even more enticing. The other musicians on that recording were Jerry Meehan on bass, Richard Causon on piano and Hammond B3 and guitarist Hal Lindes. Gary Moore also made an appearance on one track.

Sergei was funding the whole thing but wouldn't pay for accommodation as everyone lived in England except me, so I had to figure out where to stay. I called Belinda Volpelier Pierrot, whose son Ben was the singer in Curiosity Killed The Cat, an old friend and she said she'd look into it for me. A couple of days later, she told me she had a friend who was selling a house which was currently vacant. It was a gorgeous Georgian terraced house just off Edgware Road. This was the first time I'd spent an extended stay in London as the only time I go to England is to see Joannie in Ramsgate.

Anyway, each morning I would go to Starbucks on Edgware Road. to get coffee and a newspaper. I have to say how shocked I was hardly hearing English spoken anywhere in the neighbourhood. It was also hard to find an English paper – there were so many foreign language journals I had to dig deep to find one that I could understand.

We recorded the album at Sphere studios in south London close to Battersea so it wasn't a long trip from the house to the studio. Mostly

I would have a car pick me up but sometimes I would take a bus and sit upstairs just to take in the old and new sights. The sessions were fun and a pleasure playing with that great bunch of guys. At one point Sergei asked me to co-write a song in the style of 'Maggie May', which was easy for me as I must have played it about two thousand times! I was promised a 'buy out' but wouldn't you know it never came through... the whole thing lasted about three weeks and was a joy to be part of it.

The following year in 2009, Warner released new DVD and Blu-ray versions of the film of *Woodstock: 3 Days of Peace & Music* in honour of the 40th anniversary of that extraordinary festival. Along with much celebrated footage, the DVD also featured previously unseen songs performed by the Who, Joe Cocker, Canned Heat, Joan Baez and Country Joe and the Fish, as well as some new documentaries. The soundtrack was to be digitally remastered for the new release but unfortunately... or perhaps fortunately for me, Hendrix's infamous rendition of 'The Star Spangled Banner' couldn't be remastered due to extraneous background noise that was unable to be erased. A friend of mine asked me to record a version of the anthem as if played by Hendrix. I used a Strat and a Marshall amp and a phaser to obtain Jimi's sound. I copied Hendrix's solo – note for note. When I heard it back I couldn't tell which was the great man's original recording or my version. It was quite an honour to be asked to replicate such an iconic performance from one of my heroes. An absolute labour of love.

I was having a year off from working with Johnny when I received a call from the late producer Andrew Tribe, who in the past had acted for me in a royalty deal with Universal Publishing. He was putting together a band called Apart from Rod, which Jim Cregan had told me about. The band consisted of a couple of the original members of Rod's band and who had also written some of his songs. There was Jim, another Rod alumnus Gary Grainger, Pat Davey on bass, Harry James (drums), Sam Tanner (keyboards and vocals) and Robert Hart (Bad Company) on lead vocals.

I got myself to London quite sharpish to rehearse with them and was very pleasantly surprised to find how great the new guys were. It really sounded like the old Rod Stewart group. We worked on the songs for a couple of days and were then ready to take to the road. Gary missed the last days of rehearsals and then decided for some reason or other he did not want to be part of the group. So we had just Jim and me on guitars. I was staying with Jim at a guest house in Surrey he rented from a friend, Sara Nutell. It was winter and I remember it being freezing when I had to go outside for my morning tea and cigarettes. Andrew used to come over occasionally to talk about the future of the group and in the evening would ask me if I had some 'antifreeze' (aka vodka, as it doesn't freeze). I always did. Andrew had great plans for the group and I was told there would be a tour in the summer, but I could only be with them for a few weeks as I had to be in Paris in March for a TV special with Johnny.

The first show I played with them I believe was at The Boom Boom Club, at Sutton United's football ground – a slightly different football venue than the Stade de France! Just before we went on I suddenly realised I didn't have any eyeliner. Sara scoured the audience until she found me some that a fan generously gave her. It was dark brown, not black as I would normally use but beggars can't be choosers. Yes I know… I'm an old tart! The show went really well to a packed audience and I thought this could be something I could do when I wasn't working with Johnny. The band was really very good, we had a lot of fun and it was great to play those songs which I hadn't broached for years. One review made me laugh; 'Robin Le Mesurier resembles the love child of Keith Richards and Ronnie Wood.' Ha!

Eventually I had to get back to LA and start rehearsing for Johnny's TV show in Paris. It happened to be my birthday on the day of the shoot, and as we walked on to the stage the entire audience, who had clearly been tipped off by the show's host, sang 'Happy Birthday' to me. It was touching but I felt a little embarrassed. Johnny and Laeticia had organised a party for me after the show, which I had no idea about, but it was very sweet and lovely of them and so unexpected.

Later on that year there were more dates for Apart From Rod. Robert had left the group by then but was replaced by a very talented singer, Jim Stapely. So I was back again later in the summer for a short tour, including a festival in Germany. It was absolutely pouring when we got there and our poor crew had to set up in those horrible conditions. We were to go on late afternoon and as luck would have it the rain stopped and the sun was shining brilliantly. The weird thing was that, as soon as we finished, it came down in buckets again. Talk about luck! Anyway, I decided that would be my last stint with that group because although it was a fun gig it wasn't financially that rewarding. Since then the name of the band has been changed to Cregan' And Co. I think mostly to try and get away from being sometimes thought of as being a tribute band, which was definitely not the case.

I was back on the road again with Johnny in 2012 and there was one special concert that I'll always remember with huge affection. Johnny had never played in the UK before and I'd never played at the Albert Hall before, although I'd been there many times as an audience member, seeing various groups over the years. We were scheduled to do two shows at the iconic venue.

During every show there is always a 'band' song so Johnny or 'the singer' as I call him, can get a change of clothes. Normally Amy Keys, one of our backing singers, calls out to the audience in French, 'Hello, how are you doing?' But on the second night when she started her little speech, I took the microphone from her and asked the packed house, 'Wait a minute, is there anyone here who speaks English?' The whole place erupted with cries of 'YEEEEEEEEES!' I was pretty surprised because although this was London there is a huge French population living in the city. Anyway I continued, 'That's great, thanks. This is my home town and I was born only about a mile from here. This is my first time playing here too.' I received a wonderfully warm reception with cheers and applause. It was lovely.

But, the one thing that really got to me was when we played our version of 'Hey Joe', the famous Jimi Hendrix tune. Jimi and Johnny were friends in the sixties and the song was released in England and France, during the same week, with Johnny singing French lyrics. Both renditions actually went to number one. Standing in my usual position of stage right it suddenly occurred to me while I was playing the now famous guitar intro, I was standing in almost the very same position on stage where he had appeared and played this famous song. I had come to see Hendrix at the Albert Hall and now here I was standing where he stood. It was a very haunting and spiritual experience for me and still gives me goosebumps thinking about it to this day.

Music critics in the UK can be notorious for slamming almost every show they review. But in our case it was quite the opposite. Every single journalist who wrote about the shows we did there were so full of praise it was almost embarrassing. Almost! This from the *Independent*, 'although Hallyday has sold in excess of 110 million records across Europe, few if any of those sales occurred in Britain... he certainly doesn't struggle to fill the place, with charisma at least, boasting the easy assurance that comes with a lifetime of commanding stages. It's hard not to be charmed by Hallyday himself – not least for the way, when he walks amongst the fans, he bestows his favours not on the youngest ladies, but upon those whose dedication is more deeply founded. A gentleman and a rocker.'

I have had a link with former members of The Faces for many years having worked and socialised with them for much of my career, but had never actually been 'A Face'. This was to change in January 2015 at Rod's seventieth birthday party in LA on a glorious night. He was throwing a big bash at which there was a 'forties' dress code. Easy for the guys as all we needed was a dinner jacket, but for all the girls it was much more difficult. Wigs, hats, the right shoes etc. but with a lot of thought and effort in the end of course everyone looked fabulous! There were so many people there, lots of old friends who I hadn't seen for ages. Many flew in for the party, Rod's brothers, their wives and his sister Mary who I've always loved. And also Ronnie Wood and Kenney Jones from The Faces – a group I dreamed of being in the same way as Ronnie dreamed of being a Rolling Stone, which of course he has been for the last forty years.

Jules and a couple of other people told me to bring a guitar, so I did, just in case there might be a jam later. There was an orchestra playing all the great standards from the era and Rod got up and did a few numbers with them. There were also some spare amplifiers for 'guest' guitarists. Towards the end of the evening, Rod got on the stage and said something like, 'Ok, let's give this a go.' Kenney was already moving to the drums, Conrad Korsch (Rod's bass player), and Chuck Kentis (his keyboard player) were taking to the stage too. Ronnie gave me a look as to say, 'Come on, let's go.' So we both strolled up there and plugged in to our amps, tuned up a little and off we went. We played 'Losing You', 'Stay With Me' and 'Sweet Little Rock and Roller.' It was a little messy but loads of fun! After we left the stage Rod came up to me and said, 'Well, that's it, you're a 'Face' now.' I was blown away! Another dream had come true.

Once 'a Face'… from left – Ronnie Wood, Sir Rod, Conrad Korsch and Kenny Jones.

Nine months later I was on stage with the Faces again – this time playing in front of a large audience. Every year Kenney Jones and his wife Jayne hold a polo game and a concert for their prostate cancer charity at Hurtwood Park Polo Club in Surrey. Kenney had the disease but happily recovered. It was decided that The Faces would play a fortieth reunion gig there. I flew to London a few days before the gig and we had rehearsed on three occasions for a just couple of hours each day. But it all came together pretty well.

There were other acts on the bill that day and evening. Steve Harley played with Jim Cregan, Chris Jagger and Molly Marriot (Steve Marriot's daughter), Midge Ure, Paul Carrack and a few others. Sadly The Faces' original keyboard player Ian McLagan passed away in 2014 and Ronnie Lane was long gone. So Konrad was on bass and Sam Tanner and Josh Phillips on keys. In fact the show also was a tribute to Ian and Ronnie. By the time we went on it was very cold and I thought my fingers would lock up! We played only for about fifty minutes and it seemed to go by so fast. But it was a blast actually being in The Faces.

In August 2016, Rod… sorry… Sir Rod hosted a party to celebrate the knighthood he received in the Queen's Birthday Honours, which he and Penny called 'the knighthood Sunday dinner'. The menu was emblazoned with a crown and the Union Jack colours, and we sat down to 'Noble Prawn Cocktail' and 'Royal Lamb Shank'. It was only fitting that Rod should celebrate his with a Sunday lunch. The tradition of a Sunday roast continued wherever has lived and wherever the band were playing and I'm glad to say I've been a regular attendee.

The usual suspects at Rod's knighthood Sunday dinner (PENNY LANCASTER)

During the Rod Stewart tours we usually had Sundays off and wherever we were – sometimes well off the beaten track – I would call a local restaurant and ask them if they could do us a roast. It had to be roast lamb, roast potatoes, veg and all the trimmings. Quite often I would call ahead and give them the menu and invariably I also had to tell them how to cook it (one of the many things I learned from my mother). Most times they got it right and we'd have a scrumptious meal,

185

including mint sauce! We looked forward to those nights immensely. But, strangely enough, when we were in New Zealand, roast lamb was not to be found at any of the hotels. Lamb… New Zealand? What was all that about? Funny old world.

I love to cook, much influenced by Mum and Bruce Copp. Rod and Penny came around for dinner on one occasion and, although I say so myself, I prepared a fabulous lamb shank. It was so good that Rod offered me money to set up a restaurant. That's not going to happen – for a number of reasons – mainly that it is much too much hard work. A group of us have continued this Sunday dinner institution, which has continued in LA for over thirty years and there are some stalwart members, nearly all are ex-pats.

Annie Challis, who was originally from Surrey, began her career in this business working at Capital Radio in London, both as a producer and broadcaster with Kenny Everett and Gerald Harper. She then started her own PR Company and she was introduced to Rod by Elton John. Annie moved to Beverly Hills to work with Rod and she was brilliant with helping me obtain my green card. We would also sometimes go carol singing – which was blast as people would open the door to a rag tag bunch of carollers and witness Rod warbling, 'God Rest Ye Merry Gentlemen'. Annie finally became fed up with so much travelling, gave up PR and went into the property business. She still lives in LA and is very much a part of our ex-pat gatherings.

Lionel Conway is a very good mate, who I have known for years. Lionel is a music publisher, who now represents Tom Waits. He is a proper cockney – actually born within the sound of Bow Bells. Lionel left school at fifteen and worked with musician Sidney Bron (actress Eleanor Bron's father) before joining up with the legendary Dick James. I first met Lionel in 1978 when I was recording with Lion. We had Sunday night dinners, a weekly event when each of us took it in turn to host and cook. There used to be a football game and we would meet in the Cock and Bull on Sunset Boulevard for drinks. We used to drive home half cut, which was foolish – luckily no-one was killed.

In the early 1980s restaurateur Eddie Kerkhofs, who I mentioned earlier, used to host Sunday night dinners at his place and we usually had English roasts. Some of the guests were musicians and most of them were hard of hearing after playing so many live gigs surrounded by booming speakers! After dinner we would listen to albums but Eddie's stereo system wasn't the greatest and his speakers were attached to rafters close to the ceiling. Ronnie Wood was always asking Eddie to turn up the volume, which he did. He lived in an 'A' frame house and was built with rafters which, if you lifted yourself up to and hung from them, you could put one ear right next to the speakers. One night we cranked up the volume so loud, the system blew up and so Eddie had to use a small transistor radio for the music. It wasn't much use but better than nothing, although Ronnie wasn't impressed.

I still meet regularly with Eddie who ran Le Dôme for twenty-seven years and recently told me this story; Richard Pryor and Sammy Davis Jr used to come in together to eat at the restaurant. Pryor was a vegetarian but Sammy's favourite dish was 'Pig's Knuckle' which he referred to as, 'the usual'. All the waiting staff knew what he wanted when he ordered 'the usual'. On one occasion Richard said to Sammy, 'I've had it watching you eat that pig dish. This time, if order that and eat it while I'm sitting opposite you at the table, I'm walking out.' Sammy replied, 'Well that's what I'm having. That is my usual. But, you don't need to walk out. You don't need to watch me eat the dish.' Pryor asked him, 'Well, how is that going to work?' Sammy told him, 'Just sit under the table. It will take me ten to fifteen minutes to finish the knuckle and when I've finished I'll knock on the top of the table and you can come out.' That's exactly what happened. Pryor sat under the table and when Sammy had finished, he rapped it on the table top. Richard Pryor came out and sat down as if nothing had happened! I would love to have seen the faces of the diners at nearby tables.

Jules and I are very happy in our West Hollywood home which we share with our dogs – sometimes they are more demanding than kids. Unfortunately Jules and I haven't been able to have children. If there's one thing I miss, I think it's not being able to have children. God knows I've tried! The sad thing about my being childless, is that when my time is up there will be no one to carry on my name, of which I'm very proud and which goes back to eleventh century in Normandy. We did talk about adoption at one stage and Johnny and Laeticia who have adopted two children Jade and Joy from Vietnam offered to help, but the timing never seemed right. I guess it just wasn't meant to be.

Jules and I and love each other very much and look after each other.

Unfortunately Jules has had to undergo a quite a lot of surgery and I've become a part time nurse – and hopefully a little more sympathetically than my mum had to play in as Matron in *Carry on Nurse*. Jules is always very flattering about me and thinks that I 'always do the right thing.' She recently said of me, 'He's safe, not a worrier, and doesn't get stressed. Robin is sweet, has a tender heart, and has so many good friends.' I know she worries that I'm not one to open up and when I'm quiet, she sometimes thinks I may be angry or upset but I never am!

My father-in law passed away in 2015, which was very difficult for Jules and I. John Bennici died in Phoenix, Arizona, while I was working with Johnny in Toulouse and we were just about to do a show when I heard the news. John and I had become very close through the years that I'd known him and he had always treated me like a son. Johnny and the band, especially Geoff, were very supportive, but it was a very difficult show for me to do. I was just going through the motions, almost robotically for two and a half hours. All I could think about was how Jules must be hurting, and the fact that I was so far away made me feel so helpless. All I could really think about was what Jules must be going through while I was trying to do my best in front of an audience.

Long after their deaths, my parents continue to have a huge influence on me and the way I live my life. My character and outlook were shaped by their kindness, generosity and tolerant natures. I have been greatly influenced by their belief in good manners – dad always maintained that the two most important words in the English language were 'please' and 'thank you' and I agree. My friend Sherry Daly believes I have been 'family trained' and I think she is absolutely right.

And of course theirs is also a physical presence; the films and television shows in which they featured are never off the screen. Their lives have been immortalised on the printed page – Joannie has written a couple of books about Dad and there have been biographies of both Mum and Dad. Andy Merriman's *Hattie* was the basis of the film of the same name, first broadcast on BBC television in January, 2011. It's one thing seeing your parents regularly on screen, but another to have their real lives under scrutiny and depicted by actors.

I was so thrilled that Ruth Jones was cast as my mum and I met with her at a restaurant in Soho. I admitted that I was very nervous about meeting her and she surprisingly said she was equally nervous. She was absolutely fantastic and really captured Mum's character. I was initially disappointed that Bill Nighy wasn't playing Dad, but was delighted with Robert Bathurst's performance. Funnily enough Bill Nighy played Dad's part of Sergeant Wilson part in the new *Dad's Army* film.

My life so far has been like a roller coaster, but saying that, a really fantastic roller coaster, one you'd like to ride over and over again and again. I've been so lucky so far, and many times being in the right place at the right time helps. Also, a little nepotism doesn't go amiss either. It's a weird thing which applies to most writers, musicians or entertainers – none of them 'retire'. And occasionally I'm asked, 'When are you going to stop?' I always reply, 'Never!' Why should I stop doing what I love to do, writing songs, recording and my biggest love, playing live in front of an audience, big or small? I will never retire.

Also, I've been very lucky health-wise, I've never spent a night in a hospital, though when I was very young I had to go to the emergency room for an accident that happened at home; the washing machine's hose broke and I got scalded on my feet – but that's it. I've never broken a bone, and with all the bad and sometimes illegal substances I've put in my body I seem to have come through all that without any problems. Every year I have a complete check up from my doctor… and feel like the man who jumped off the Empire State building and was heard to call out at each level, 'So far so good!'

Sometimes I think of Ronnie Wood, Keith Richards and a few others and ask myself, 'If they can keep going, why can't I?' Perhaps it's just good genes. Quite recently, I've lost a good many friends, and I still wake in the morning wondering how I'm still on this earth and feeling fine. I think it's because I have a lot more to accomplish before it's my departure time. I couldn't imagine not working anymore (though I really don't consider what I do is working), it's a great feeling being creative and getting feedback from people who love what you give to them. Playing live is like a 'domino effect', the more you give to the audience, the more they give back to you. And, it's a great high. Better than any drug.

It's obvious to me that I have had 'Someone to Watch Over Me' as the Gershwin song goes because I really have had a 'Charmed Life'. Be it in rock 'n' roll or otherwise. I've met the most interesting people, been given the best advice (for the most part), and had a wonderful time doing what I love to do.

I've also been fortunate to work with a host of many other amazing artists and with two of the greatest singers on the planet, Rod Stewart and Johnny Hallyday, who I've been with for over two decades and the longest serving musician he's ever had. We're recording a new album in LA soon and I'm currently writing some songs. Johnny once told me, 'I'll die on stage.' I certainly hope he doesn't while I'm with him! But I understand that, with his love of being on stage and in front of an audience. I feel the same way.

If I had to live my life over again, I don't think I would change that much. Of course I've made mistakes, but we learn from them, and hopefully don't repeat them. Looking back to when I was a young child and Peter Greenwell gave me my first guitar, I learnt very soon that that instrument held my future. I never thought about being famous, just a guitar player. It's weird these days, because if you ask young people what they want to be later in life, so many say, 'I want to be famous.' I'm sure that answer is generated by what they see and hear in the media. Sad really. Initially Mum and Dad had both been concerned about music being the right career choice for me because it's so insecure. But they both became immensely proud that I was doing what I loved to do and was able to earn a living from it. I'm just as proud that I've been able to survive in this business and although there is inevitably some competitiveness between musicians, I've never felt jealous of the success of others.

I have to thank everyone who has supported me on my journey, you know who you are, and especially to my close family, what's left of them, and hope to be around long enough to tell more tales before I leave this planet. I always believe the glass is always half full and not half empty – an old adage but something I believe in… especially if it's a vodka martini!

ACKNOWLEDGEMENTS

I'm very grateful to the following people for their contributions and assistance with the book.

Andi Banks, Bernie Boyle, Pete Buckland, Zally Caws, Annie Challis, Lionel Conway, Bruce Copp, Jim Cregan, Sherry Daly, Geoff Dugmore, Britt Ekland, Kelly Emberg, Robin Gray, Johnny Hallyday, John Paul Jacques, Eddie Kerkhofs, Chris Kimsey, Penny Lancaster, Alan Merrill, Joel Merriman, Joan Le Mesurier, Robin Le Mesurier (Bun) Richard McNeff, Guy Pratt, Tim Renton, Shirley Roden, Joanne Russell, Kevin Savigar, Victoria Sellers, John Sinclair, Sir Rod Stewart CBE, Bernie Taupin, Gina Vaisey, Tad Wadhams, Steve Webb, Ronnie Wood and Patrick Woodroffe OBE.

Thanks to all at the Book Guild especially Jeremy Thompson, Jack Wedgbury and Sarah Taylor.

To Cathy Vivier for being my number one fan… apart from Jules, of course.

And finally to Andy Merriman for all his help.